ellan Strait

San Sebastian Bay

Atlantic Ocean

**Isla
rande**

**Isla
Grande**

Thetis Bay

Good Success Bay

Le Maire Strait

Staten Isl.

rande

Beagle Channel

◄ Wulaia

Navarin Isl.

Murray Narrows

Nassau
Bay

Goree Road

Cape Horn→

← Wollaston Isl.

Hermite Isl. ———→

Cape Horn

DARWIN IN TIERRA DEL FUEGO
1832, 1833, 1834

DARWIN IN
TIERRA DEL FUEGO

Tierra del Fuego

DARWIN IN
TIERRA DEL FUEGO

ANNE CHAPMAN

IMAGO MUNDI
BUENOS AIRES

Chapman, Anne
    Darwin in Tierra del Fuego - 1a ed. - Buenos Aires : Imago Mundi, 2006.
    180 p.; 23x15 cm.

    ISBN 950-793-049-3

    1. Etnografía. I. Título
    CDD 305.8

Fecha de catalogación: 07/04/2006

Ediciones Imago Mundi
Av. Independencia 3018 - Tel.: (011) 4932-3890
C1225AAZ Ciudad Autónoma de Buenos Aires
E–mail: odilonlibros@fibertel.com.ar

Diseño, diagramación y armado: Gráfica Puntosur
E–mail: graficapuntosur@fibertel.com.ar – Tel.: (011) 4954–7498

CONTENTS

ACKNOWLEDGEMENTS   XIII

PREFACE   XV

CHAPTER I
DARWIN IS CHOSEN BY FITZ-ROY TO ACCOMPANY
HIM ON THE SECOND BEAGLE VOYAGE: 1831   1

1.   THE FIRST BEAGLE VOYAGE: 1826-1830   1
2.   DARWIN, AS THE CANDIDATE FOR THE SECOND VOYAGE: 1831   4
3.   FITZ-ROY AND DARWIN MEET   5
4.   TWO OF DARWIN'S STRONGLY HELD CONVICTIONS   6
5.   WHO WERE THE FUEGIAN INDIANS?   7
6.   THE THREE FUEGIANS DARWIN MET: 1830-1831   8
7.   DARWIN WAS NOT A RACIST   9
8.   THE PARADIGM OF CULTURAL / SOCIAL EVOLUTION   10

CHAPTER 2
THE SECOND BEAGLE VOYAGE BEGINS: 1831-32   13

1.   PREPARATIONS FOR DEPARTURE: SEPTEMBER-DECEMBER: 1831   13
2.   THE CREW AND THE SUPERNUMERARIES   14
3.   WESTERN CIVILIZATION ARRIVES AT A CROSSROAD   17
4.   OFF TO TIERRA DEL FUEGO   18
5.   DARWIN'S AND FITZ-ROY'S PORTRAITS OF THE THREE FUEGIANS:
     YORK, FUEGIA AND JEMMY   18

6. THE "OENS-MEN" (THE SELK'NAM) — 24
7. DARWIN'S FIRST EXPERIENCES WITH THE FUEGIANS,
    IN GOOD SUCCESS BAY: DECEMBER 17-20, 1832 — 24
8. THE MAIN ENCOUNTERS: DECEMBER 18 — 25
9. THE LAST BRIEF ENCOUNTERS: DECEMBER 19 AND 20 — 30
10. DARWIN RECALLS HIS FIRST IMPRESSIONS OF THE FUEGIANS — 30
11. IMAGINE FOR A MOMENT... — 32
12. DARWIN'S "GOOD SUCCESS EXCURSIONS": DECEMBER 19-20 — 33
13. ON TOWARDS CAPE HORN: CHRISTMAS AND THE LAST WEEK OF 1832 — 35

CHAPTER 3

DARWIN'S "MEDITATIONS" (MY TERM) ABOUT THE FUEGIANS

37

1. THE WOLLASTON ISLANDERS
    "THE MOST ABJECT AND MISERABLE CREATURES..." — 39
2. THEIR HUT, A "HAYCOCK" — 40
3. THEIR FIRE — 40
4. THEY LIVED "CHIEFLY ON SHELLFISH..." — 42
5. "THEY KILL AND DEVOUR THEIR OLD WOMEN..." — 46
6. THEIR LANGUAGE (ANOTHER SERIOUS MISTAKE DARWIN MADE) — 49
7. "WHEN AT WAR [THEY] ARE CANNIBALS..." — 50
8. BURIALS IN CAVES AND FORESTS — 52
9. NO RELIGION — 54
10. NO CHIEFS, NO GOVERNMENT — 56
11. "NO FEELING OF HOME" — 58
12. "NO DOMESTIC AFFECTION" — 60
13. "THE HUSBAND IS TO THE WIFE A BRUTAL MASTER" — 60
14. "THEIR SKILL [IS LIKE]... THE INSTINCT OF ANIMALS" — 63
15. BUT WHY DID THE FUEGIANS SETTLE IN THIS END OF NO- WHERE? — 64
16. DARWIN'S LEGACY: A MISERABLE PEOPLE "FIT" A MISERABLE COUNTRY — 64

CHAPTER 4

DARWIN MEETS THE YAHGANS AT HOME: 1833

67

1. THE WORST STORM EVER ENCOUNTERED: JANUARY 1 - 13 — 67
2. VIA BEAGLE CHANNEL IN A CARAVAN:
    DARWIN IS PLEASED: JANUARY 19 - 22 — 69
3. DARWIN MEETS THE YAMANA (YAHGAN) AT HOME — 71
4. JEMMY'S BAD NEIGHBORS: DARWIN "MUCH AFRAID..." — 72
5. NO-MAN'S LAND — 74
6. JEMMY'S FRIENDS — 74
7. YORK, THE JEALOUS SUITOR — 75
8. JEMMY'S FEAR OF THE OENS-MEN — 76
9. AN ADVANCE PARTY ARRIVES "LIKE SO MANY DEMONIACS..." — 77
10. DOWN MURRAY NARROWS, "A SCENE WHICH CARRIED ONE'S
    THOUGHTS TO THE SOUTH SEA ISLANDS" — 78

11. THE FIRST DAY IN WULAIA, EVERYONE IS PLEASED: JANUARY 23   80
12. FITZ-ROY MARKS OFF A NO-TRESPASSING ZONE   80
13. THE WORK BEGINS   82
14. THE SECOND DAY, JEMMY IS REUNITED WITH HIS FAMILY   83
15. JEMMY, TOMMY, HARRY AND BILLY BUTTON   84
16. YORK TELLS DARWIN SOME STARTLING NEWS   84
17. THE THIRD DAY IN WULAIA, GOOD NEIGHBORS RETURN: JANUARY 25   85
18. TOO MANY "STRANGERS": JANUARY 26   86
19. THE BATHING SCENE   86
20. PRACTICE SHOOTING BEFORE DARK   . 87
21. THE OLD MEN ARE NOT SO FRIENDLY   87
22. DARWIN AND FITZ-ROY ARE ANXIOUS: JANUARY 27   88
23. THE LAST MORNING IN WULAIA, FOR NOW   89
24. FITZ-ROY INVITES DARWIN TO SAIL DOWN "GLACIER LANE": JANUARY 28...   90
25. THE HERO OF THE DAY   92
26. DARWIN ON THE MAP   93
27. A NOT-SO-FRIENDLY ENCOUNTER   94
28. GOOD TIDINGS IN WULAIA: FEBRUARY 6   95
29. THE "BAD MEN" HAD COME   96
30. DEPARTURE FROM WULAIA, FOR NOW;
     DARWIN HAS A SECOND THOUGHT   97
31. FITZ-ROY RETURNS TO WULAIA WITHOUT DARWIN: FEBRUARY 14   99
32. MEANWHILE, THE "STRANGERS"   99
33. THE FIRST DEPARTURE FROM TIERRA DEL FUEGO:
     LATE FEBRUARY 1833   100
34. ELSEWHERE, THE FOLLOWING ELEVEN MONTHS:
     EARLY MARCH 1833 TO LATE JANUARY 1834   100

CHAPTER 5
DARWIN'S LAST VISIT IN TIERRA DEL FUEGO: 1834

                                                                     103

1. HE ENTERS MAGELLAN STRAIT AND
    MEETS THE TEHUELCHE INDIANS: JANUARY 26-30   103
2. DARWIN'S "ADVENTURE" NEAR PORT FAMINE: FEBRUARY 2 -10   105
3. BACK THROUGH THE MAGELLAN STRAIT;
    DARWIN SIGHTS THE OENS-MEN: FEBRUARY 10 -13   105
4. WHALES OFF THE NORTH COAST OF ISLA GRANDE: FEBRUARY 14- 21   106
5. DARWIN ADMIRES "FINE TALL MEN..." IN THETIS BAY: LATE FEBRUARY   108
6. THE WOLLASTON ISLANDERS, THE MOST "MISERABLE" OF ALL THE FUEGIANS   108
7. AMUSING CONTACTS ON THE WAY BACK TO WULAIA   110
8. FAREWELL WULAIA: MARCH 5-6,1834   112
9. JEMMY'S PREFERENCE   115
10. MATTHEWS' PREFERENCE   115
11. YORK'S AND FUEGIA'S PREFERENCE   115
12. THE OENS-MEN HAD ATTACKED   116
13. FITZ-ROY'S FAREWELL TO JEMMY   117

Contents

13. Fitz-Roy's farewell to Jemmy   117
14. Darwin's farewell to Jemmy   118
15. The expedition carries on...   118
16. Farewell Alakalufs   120
17. The "destiny" of the Alakaluf   121
18. And the Yahgan...   121

Chapter 6
Back in England   127

1. Home at last   127
2. Darwin's recollections of the
   Fuegians and the Beagle Voyage: 1871 and 1876   128
3. My homage to Darwin   130
4. Fitz-Roy's contributions and "destiny"   130
5. And the *Beagle*   131

Notes   133

Bibliography   147

Lists of illustrations   155

ACKNOWLEDGEMENTS

This text was completed and published in Buenos Aires, in March and April 2006. First of all, I wish to thank Catalina Saugy, member of the Instituto Nacional de Antropología (INAPL), for locating a very resourceful editor, Alejandro Falco, the director of Imago Mundi. Catalina also assisted me in many other ways. Another friend, Beatriz Seibel, helped me a great deal with the preface. A North American editor, Lea Fletcher, corrected the nearly final text: "nearly," because any errors the reader may find are probably in the additions I made later. Veronica del Valle worked intensely with me before going to press. In Santiago, Chile, Jorge Mery Garcia kindly sent me illustrations I very much needed. He and Silvia Contreras Quiroga were constantly attentive to the progress of this text. I am grateful to the family of the artist Eduardo Armstrong for permission to publish three illustrations of his beautiful paintings and to Alan Warren for his usual photograph of a guanaco. I am also grateful to other friends here in Buenos Aires. Soledad Gonzalez Marichal suggested that I add more data on Darwin and the Fuegians. Roxana Risco and Saul Keifman made other very helpful comments. Laila Williams has assisted me a great deal by establishing contact with the American Museum of Natural History in New York.

Actually the nucleus of this book was written previously, though in a different context, as two chapters of a fifteen-chapter text (not yet published) entitled *Cape Horn, Encounters with the Native people before and after Darwin*. During that "previous" time Janet Browne (in London) and Sandra Herbert (in Washington DC) very kindly read and commented on the two Darwin chapters. I am also grateful to Colin McEwan who gave me Janet Browne's first volume on Darwin in 1997 and to Edith Couturier who facilitated my contact with Sandra Herbert. Betty Meggers in Washington DC, and George Stocking Jr. (by E mail) gave me very relevant advice concerning my style of writing. This entire text was carefully read by Lewis Burgess in New York, by Claude Baudez in Paris and by Mario Fonseca in Santiago. My fieldwork in Tierra del Fuego (Chile), mentioned in the preface below, was greatly aided by Mateo Martinic and other members of the Instituto de la Patagonia (Punta Arenas, Chile). The authorities in Puerto Williams (Navarin Island, Chile) and the personnel of the museum dedicated to Martin Gusinde greatly facilitated my work with the four descendants of the Yahgans who spoke their native language. Their testimonies were very important for the long (unpublished) text. For this shorter one, Cristina Calderón, her sister Ursula, and Ermelina Acuña gave me important data on the last Yahgan ceremony, that took place about 1933, mentioned below in Chapter 3. The Centre National de la Recherche Scientifique (Paris) financed my long periods of fieldwork and of research on the Fuegians. I am also thinking about my late brother, Theodore Chapman, who so unfailingly admired Charles Darwin, and was happy to collaborate by sending me articles and reviews concerning him.

PREFACE

This text has been written for readers interested in young Darwin, his great "adventure" in Tierra del Fuego, his most intense and prolonged contact with natives during the long Beagle voyage. I propose to highlight his almost day-to-day relations with Captain Robert Fitz-Roy and with the Fuegian natives. Why did he write about them with such utter derision, despite his friendship for Jemmy Button, one of the Fuegians who accompanied him on this voyage? I propose several answers to this question.

I have concentrated on working with the last few descendants of the Fuegians. No anthropologist had interviewed them for forty years, since Father Martin Gusinde spent long months with them between 1919 and 1923 and eventually published his historical and ethnographic opus, originally published in German and now available in Spanish (see Bibliography below). Since 1964, I have returned to Tierra del Fuego countless times, interviewing the few who had remained. I recorded their memories and life histories and published several books, articles, many chants and made two films, the first in collaboration with Ana Montés. I also explored uninhabited areas of Tierra del Fuego, including Staten Island and Good Success Bay, where Darwin first met the Fuegians in December 1832. I was particularly keen on visiting the other places that he had written about in his Voyage of the Beagle, mainly the Cape Horn area and Wulaia, on Navarin Island. Thanks to the Chilean Navy I was able to do so while making the second film, called Homage to the Yahgans, in 1987 and 1988.

Young Darwin emerges as charismatic, dynamic, congenial, absorbed in the science of nature. He vividly recalled the native Fuegians near the end of his life, in 1876, though he erroneously assumed that they were cannibals - of the worst sort imaginable. Jemmy Button, a younger man, presents the figure of a Fuegian very attached to his "countrymen" though at times furiously angry at them, very fond of his British friends, though unwilling to go back to England. He acquires the allure of a symbol for the present and the future: a person in love with his "country" who simultaneously welcomes the outside world, in his case England.

I first went to Tierra del Fuego in 1964-65 as a member of a French archaeological team. I was eager to meet Lola Kiepja, who was the last Fuegian who had actually lived as her ancestors (until she was about thirty years old). She was a Selk'nam, some eight-five or ninety years old when I met her. By then her twelve children and all the adults of her generation had passed away. I was impressed by her vivacity and her willingness to share her memory with me of the Selk'nam "world" that no longer existed. I returned in 1966 and stayed beside her during most of three months, where she lived alone on the Indian reservation, Tierra del Fuego, Argentina. She was very happy to listen to her own voice as I recorded the chants she recalled, finally over a hundred, most of which have been published. Lola died a few months later, on October 9, 1966.[1] She was and remains the source of my inspiration. After her death I became determined to do my utmost to work with the descendants of the Fuegians who had some memories of their ancient cultures: the Selk'nam (also called Onas), as well as the Yahgans whom Darwin met in Tierra del Fuego during his Beagle voyage.

I was really discouraged when I read the following words by a highly regarded scholar, specialist of Darwin, Peter J. Bowler. "Unfortunately, the non-specialist may well find himself or herself daunted by the sheer quantity of the Darwin industry's output." Janet Browne, the author of the most extensive biography of Darwin, asserted that more has been written about him than any other scientist.[2] Moreover, Darwin's own writings cover fifty years of his life from 1832 until his death in 1882. They are vast and varied. The extent of his interests and talents is overwhelming. He was a keen observer of nature, alert to the expertise of animal breeders and guardians in the London zoos, and to the publications of a great variety of scientists, very attentive to the behavior young children, even adults as well as animals, an experimentalist, and a philosophical theoretician. His vast research and his intellectual courage have inspired generations of scientists and made him the center of controversy today and probably for a long time to come. The eminent biologist Ernst Mayr, an undisputed authority on Darwin, affirmed that his impact on the thinking of modern man "surpasses that of all other scientists and philosophers." Bowler phrased Darwin's contributions as the "watershed separating modern culture from the traditional roots of Western Thought."[3]

Volumes have been written about Darwin's scientific work and very well documented books and articles concern his childhood, his youth, his Beagle voyage, his family life in Down, near London, his innumerable contacts with friends and scientists, how he confronted the problems that resulted from his unorthodox scientific work, etc. However, very little has been published on the details of his three visits to Tierra del Fuego, from mid-December 1832 to early March 1833 and twice in 1834. This text is meant to fill this lacuna, focusing on his contacts with the Fuegians.

The notes are for the readers who want to go beyond the text. They are not only bibliographic references, many are meant to orient the curious reader and the student interested in the life and works of Darwin. The Fuegian natives he encountered in Tierra del Fuego are not well known, even to some anthropologists, so I detail the most available publications about them in the notes: for the Yahgan-Yamana with whom Darwin had most contact, as well as the other three groups: the Alakaluf, the Haush and the Selk'nam (or Onas). The book has been written on these two levels (text and notes) to make it available to a broad spectrum of readers, as an introduction to Darwin and to the Fuegians.

NOTES

1. For Lola Kiepja see Chapman 2003b Chapter 1.
2. Bowler 1988: 25; Browne 1995: p. X.
3. Mayr 1988: 183, 194; Bowne 1988: 174.

CHAPTER I

DARWIN IS CHOSEN BY FITZ-ROY TO ACCOMPANY HIM ON THE SECOND BEAGLE VOYAGE: 1831

1. THE FIRST BEAGLE VOYAGE :1826-1830

Captain Robert Fitz-Roy, the commander of H.M.S. *Beagle*, had returned to England from his first voyage to Tierra del Fuego in October 1830. By the summer of 1831 he was still searching for a naturalist to accompany him on his second Beagle voyage back to that "end of the world." It was standard practice at the time for the British Navy to assign the expedition's surgeon to make observations and collections as a naturalist. The surgeon, Robert Mac-Cormick, expected to perform this duty for the second voyage, in his spare time. Fitz-Roy went beyond the normal procedure and requested that a naturalist be assigned to his next expedition. Moreover, he felt the need for a companion of his own social class to share his meals and to converse with as an equal during the long voyage. Would Charles Darwin have been the scientist he became without the voyage of the *Beagle*? Fitz-Roy's initiative of contracting young Darwin may well be at the origin of what followed and should guarantee that Fitz-Roy's name be remembered, according to the late Stephan Jay Gould. [1]

1. Darwin in 1840, when he was 31 years old: painted by George Richmond. Apparently there is no portrait or sketch of Darwin during the voyage.

2. Fitz-Roy twenty-two years after the last voyage, in 1858; following his promotion to Vice-Admiral, painted by Francis Lane.

2. DARWIN AS THE CANDIDATE
FOR THE SECOND VOYAGE:1831

Darwin had no claim to nobility but his family's prestige, respectability and wealth sufficed as equivalent to Fitz-Roy's aristocratic heritage. Erasmus Darwin, his grandfather, a well-known physician and poet of his day, is still cited for having applied evolutionary principles in his study of "laws of organic life." His father, Robert Waring Darwin, was also a distinguished physician and his maternal uncle (and future father-in-law), Josiah Wedgwood, owned an immensely successful pottery factory, and was intellectually alert. Though Darwin had not been brought up in a strict Biblical milieu, he was raised as a Unitarian and his father had urged him to become a country parson. His uncle Josiah influenced (or convinced) his father to permit him to go the long Beagle voyage.

Darwin's two professors at Cambridge University: Adam Sedgwick and especially John Stevens Henslow highly recommended him to Fitz-Roy as a student of natural sciences. Henslow will become Darwin's monitor and his main scientific support and contact during the long voyage. He wrote many encouraging letters to Darwin and received his numerous envoys of boxes and crates containing specimens of all types and species. Darwin became known among British scientists even before the voyage had ended (in 1836), thanks to Henslow. He remained Darwin's loyal friend and supporter, through the difficult times that followed after the voyage, despite certain discrepancies concerning the origin of the life on earth.[2]

At the onset the Darwin-Fitz-Roy relation might not appear to augur well: Darwin the liberal Whig and Fitz-Roy the conservative Tory.[3] Fitz-Roy was also an ardent Christian, though at the time of the second Beagle voyage he was not inclined to interpret the Bible as the source of geological and biological knowledge. It was only after he returned from the voyage that he became a firm believer that the Bible related the truth concerning subjects that now (in 1831) he wanted a naturalist to investigate. During this second Beagle voyage, he and Darwin met in the middle of the road, though they were headed in opposite directions. They agreed on a wide range of subjects, though not on all (see below). They agreed that the human being, no matter how "savage," could progress to the level of civilized mankind. Both were convinced that missionaries could serve "as front-line agents" for implementing their transition to a Christian civilized level of being.[4]

3. FITZ-ROY AND DARWIN MEET

They met on September 5, 1831 in London and the following week sailed together to Plymouth to inspect the *Beagle*. That day, Darwin wrote to his sister Susan that he refrained from praising him "as I feel inclined to do, for you would not believe me. One thing I am certain of [,] nothing could be more open & kind than he was to me." He also expressed his youthful enthusiasm in a letter to his teacher Henslow:

> Cap. Fitzroy is every thing that is delightful, if I was to praise half so much as I feel inclined, you would say it was absurd, only once seeing him. I think he really wishes to have me. He offers me to mess with him & he will take care I have such [sic] room as is possible...You cannot imagine anything more pleasant, kind & open than Cap. Fitzroy's manners were to me. - I am sure it will be my fault, if we do not suit.[5]

Fitz-Roy had a different impression when Darwin walked into the room. He "took a dislike to him, particularly his nose; it was not the nose of a man who could endure the rigours of a voyage around the world." Fitz-Roy was known as a "devotee of the fashionable science of Physiognomy." Years afterwards Darwin recalled that he had "run a very narrow risk of being rejected, on account of the shape of my nose!" That very day, September 5, or soon afterwards, Fitz-Roy overlooked, or tried to ignore, his nose and praised him "as a young man of promising ability, extremely fond of geology, and indeed all branches of natural history." He had made up his mind, he wanted Darwin as his naturalist. He wrote to Francis Beaufort (the head hydrographic of the Admiralty): "I like what I see and hear of him, much, and I now request that you will apply for him to accompany me as a Naturalist."[6]

4. TWO OF DARWIN'S STRONGLY HELD CONVICTIONS

According to one of Darwin's sons:

> The two subjects which moved my Father perhaps more
> strongly than any others were cruelty to animals & slavery.
> His detestation of both was intense, and his indignation
> was overpowering in case of any levity or want of feeling
> on these matters.[7]

Throughout his life his love and admiration for animals, though focused on his pet dogs, included all animals from monkeys to worms. He not only admired animals and plants, he related to them and this partially explains his passion for observing them. Janet Browne explained: "...he gave human attributes to almost every species he met, including flatworms and beetles...He felt himself part of a single world united by the same kind of mental responses." This comment is very pertinent, as will become evident below.

He contributed regularly to the Royal Society for the Prevention of Cruelty to Animals and "was troubled throughout his life by the problems raised by vivisection."[8] Though his love for animals never ceased, in his later years he supported experiments on living animals as a necessity for physiological research.[9]

Not vivisection but slavery provoked a critical conflict with Fitz-Roy during the voyage. Darwin was a passionate abolitionist.

> Those who look tenderly at the slave-owner, and with a
> cold heart at the slave, never seem to put themselves into
> the position of the latter - what a cheerless prospect... pic-
> ture to yourself the chance, ever hanging over you, of your
> wife and your little children...being torn from you and sold
> like beasts to the first bidder![10]

He was appalled by the treatment of slaves he witnessed on plantations in Bahia, Brazil, during the first months of the voyage. Apparently once on March 12, 1832. Fitz-Roy became so infuriated about his criticism of a Brazilian slave-owner that he announced that they could no longer share the same quarters. Darwin thought he might be compelled to leave the ship. His objection to slavery was unfailing. After a while Fitz-Roy apologized to him though the subject came up again a while later.[11]

Janet Browne suggested that Darwin viewed the Fuegian Indians of Tierra del Fuego on a par with the African slaves and the rest of humanity. "Darwin had no foundation for believing that Negro slaves or native Fuegians were in some way closer to animals than he was... and the barrier between a state of savagery and one of civilisation was remarkably small."[12] But if the barrier was so small, between savagery and civilization, why did Darwin write about the Fuegians with such derision? Desmond and Moore paraphrased his thoughts on this subject, as disclosed in his B notebook: "Even races of people were spreading laterally *into their peculiar niches*, Jemmy Button's Fuegians into a desolate, windswept wilderness, civilised Englishmen into their factory cities."[13] Darwin put himself in the niche of the African slave but not in the Fuegian's niche. He was far more sympathetic to the Africans certainly because they had been torn from their homeland and enslaved and probably because he did not consider them to be savage cannibals, as he did the Fuegians (see below).

5. WHO WERE THE FUEGIAN INDIANS?

Darwin's Beagle voyage was of singular importance for the development of science, as nearly everyone knows. However the native people, the Fuegians, whom Darwin encountered or heard stories about are less familiar. The original inhabitants of Tierra del Fuego, the islands south of the Magellan Strait to Cape Horn, are known as four groups that spoke different languages. Their total population was estimated as approximately 10,000, before the epidemics and colonization began in the nineteenth century. Two were "canoe people," nomads of the sea: the Yamana (also known as Yahgan), and the Alakaluf (who also inhabited the archipelago north of Magellan Strait, along the Pacific Coast). The other two were called "foot people" because they were not navigators. They were the guanaco hunters who inhabited the largest island of Tierra del Fuego, the Isla Grande: the Selk'nam (also called Onas) and the Haush.[14]

Darwin encountered the Haush and the Yamana, the former in Good Success Bay and later in Thetis Bay, on the Isla Grande. He met the

7

Anne Chapman

Yamana frequently: near Cape Horn, along Beagle Channel and in Wulaia, on Navarin Island. He never met the Alakaluf or the Selk'nam "at
home." Jemmy Button told wild (though probably true) stories about
the latter, whom he called Oens-men. Darwin sighted them on a cliff
while sailing by the Isla Grande on December 17, 1832 and also from a
distance on Elizabeth Island, in the Magellan Strait, in February 1834.

He did become acquainted with three of the Fuegians Fitz-Roy had
brought to England during his first Beagle voyage. Then, in February
and March 1830, he had captured three Alakaluf in reprisal for a whaleboat stolen by the Alakaluf (though not by the three he captured). He
kidnapped another, a Yahgan, later (see below). Shortly after the *Beagle*
returned to England in October 1830, Fitz-Roy took the four young Fuegians to a comfortable lodging in Falmouth, where they were vaccinat-
ed a second time. The vaccines administered in Montevideo, late June or
early July (1830), had not taken effect. One of them, a youth called Boat
Memory, died of tuberculosis a few weeks later, in November 1830. He
was named in "memory" of the whaleboat stolen from Fitz-Roy, The
other two Alakaluf were named York Minster, a man about twenty-six at
that time, and Fuegia Basket, a girl ten or eleven years old.[15]

Darwin met the three survivors shortly before he sailed from Plymouth, on December 27, 1831. The third Fuegian, whom Darwin met,
was a Yahgan (Yamana), then a fifteen or sixteen years old lad. The
sailors called him Jemmy from the very first and as Fitz-Roy had sup-
posedly purchased him for a button, this became his last name. Ever
since he has been known as Jemmy Button. A son of the missionary
Thomas Bridges, Lucas Bridges, who knew Yahgans as his playmates
and throughout his youth, affirmed in his famous book, that it was
ridiculous to imagine that Jemmy had been purchased for a button "as
no native would have sold his child in exchange for HMS Beagle with
all it had on board."[16] His real name was Orundelico (spelt in a variety
of ways). Though he and his Alakaluf shipmates spoke different languages they understood enough of each other's to converse.

6. THE THREE FUEGIANS DARWIN MET: 1830-31

Fitz-Roy treated the three surviving Fuegians (whom he often called
his protégés) with special care and promised them that he would take

8

them back to their homeland. Early December 1830, the three protégés, accompanied by their *Beagle* friends, Master Murray and James Bennett, took a long stagecoach ride from Plymouth to Walthamstow, a small town northeast of London, whose pastor, Reverend William Wilson, agreed to receive them. They lived there for ten months in a small school for young children. The schoolmaster, Mr. Jenkens, endeavored to teach them English and the "plainer truths of Christianity." Jemmy Button and Fuegia Basket were the favorites and showed progress, York Minster less. He preferred smith's work and carpentry (which Jenkens also taught) to Bible learning and English, the essential subjects. These exotic pupils created quite a bit of excitement in Walthamstow during their stay. Visitors flocked to visit them: the neighbors, members of missionary societies, philanthropic ladies, Fitz-Roy's sister and his aristocratic friends. Most, or all, came bearing useful and not-so-useful gifts including "equipment" for a mission station, which was to be established in Tierra del Fuego. Fitz-Roy's sister was especially kind to them. Jemmy spoke of her years afterwards as "Cappen Sisser." Later Fitz-Roy accepted Reverend Wilson's suggestion that a certain Richard Matthews initiate missionary work among the Fuegians in Tierra del Fuego. Although Matthews was rather too young and inexperienced to assume the such a challenge, the recommendations concerning his character and his conduct assured Fitz-Roy that he would be capable of meeting it, besides he was the only volunteer.[17]

7. DARWIN WAS NOT A RACIST

Darwin's impressions, opinions and categorical statements made later concerning the "Fuegians" (mostly the Yamana-Yahgan) were often extremely derogatory. He placed them "in a lower state of improvement than any other part of the world."[18] He referred to them as "stunted, miserable wretches", as "miserable degraded savages," as "the most abject and miserable creature I anywhere behold" who "kill and devour their old women before they kill their dogs", and that "viewing such men, one can hardly make oneself believe that they are fellow-creature, and inhabitants of the same world."[19]

But despite such demeaning remarks, Darwin's relations to the three Fuegians, especially Jemmy Button, and others he met along Beagle

Channel and in Wulaia, were not those of a racist. Though he ridiculed the Haush Indians in Good Success Bay (see below) his indignation wasn't aroused, as it was later upon seeing Yahgans on Wollaston Island, near Cape Horn, and hearing shocking stories about their cannibalism. Moreover, he was favorably impressed by the Tehuelche Indians, called "Patagonians."

I have sought to clarify the sources of his negative judgment in terms of his experience and contacts in Tierra del Fuego with Fitz-Roy, William Low a sealer, and the Fuegians, as well as the profound influence that the cultural evolutionary ideas of his time exerted upon him. The Fuegians fit nicely into the notion, still prevalent today, that human beings as a whole have evolved from the savage simplicity of rude primitives (such as the Fuegians) to the sophisticated complexity of civilized ladies and gentlemen. [20]

8. THE PARADIGM OF CULTURAL/ SOCIAL EVOLUTION

It was first developed by British anthropologists in the mid-nineteenth century.[21] Why does it have such a long life? Burrow, who asked this question, referred to Victorian England. His analyses are valid today. In his own words:

> The Victorians often, perhaps usually...showed that man's future as a social animal was a glorious one...They do much to explain why nineteenth-century social theory should have taken the idea of social evolution as its key concept. They also help to explain the persistence of evolutionary positivism long after alternative theories had arisen on the continent.

As if he were referring to Thomas Kuhn's paradigms (first published in 1962) Burrow's added: "Theories do not automatically disappear because more sophisticated theories are put forward, at least in fields...most heavily charged hopes and beliefs of mankind."

Why assume that culture and society as a whole has "evolved" from simple primitives to the great civilizations, such as those of the Far and the Near East, of Egypt, Greece, Rome, and our industrial society?

Obviously one of the reasons stems from the idea of "global progress," progress in all spheres of life, of culture and society as a unit. I would add that "by and large" it stems from the false assumption that progress in technology, engineering, mathematics and science developed on a par with the way human beings treat and relate to each other, create universes of beliefs, literature, works of art and the like. Who is to say that the Renaissance Paintings are superior to the Cave Paintings in Europe and elsewhere? Some scientists recognize that civilized human beings are not more intelligent than the so-called savages or "cave men" (see below). This is the basis of my proposal. In other words, the progress alluded to above is not due to increasing brain capacity through the ages, but rather to a channeling of this capacity into the most vital or problem spheres of a society during a given epoch.

Recall that the great civilizations were mainly based on techniques of irrigation and other highly specialized methods of cultivation and on engineering employed in the pyramids of Egypt, as in the many other architectural "gems" of the classical world, including those of Mexico, of the Mayas and of Peru. The mathematic achievements evidenced in the Maya calendars, is another example. Technological and scientific advances also "gave birth" to our industrial - market society. The assumption was (is) that technological and scientific, including medical, progress went (goes) hand in hand with social progress, the way people relate. Much of what we admire in civilizations was and is largely due to these great innovations, the accomplishments (progress) in the different spheres of economy coupled with the philosophical expressions of a leisure class or cast. The "lower levels" of those civilizations were slavery, other systems of forced labor, mistreatment of women, tributes from captured enemy towns and people, ostracism of "untouchables" or outcasts, and the like. Our extraordinary improvements of living standards are not shared by everyone, while the distance between the haves and the have-nots increases. Nor can our even more extraordinary massacres and the suffering of millions of our fellow human beings in our concentration camps, on battlefields, in cities and towns, be forgotten. The idea of overall cultural-social progress, of "global progress," in all aspects of life, since Paleolithic times may seem incredibly naïve but it is still evident today.[22]

Janet Browne evoked Darwin's "strong commitment to the idea of progress, the theme of the age [in which he lived]." She pointed out that

11

he, like many of his contemporaries, firmly believed in progress, despite "the brutal working conditions, the exploitation of women and children" in England and elsewhere at the time. Improvement was thought to be an "inbuilt tendency" in virtually all aspects of life.[23]

The late Stephan Jay Gould, the outstanding paleontologist, a great admirer of Darwin despite his criticism of gradual transformation of the species, insisted that Darwin himself was opposed to the concept of progress as applied to biology. Gould advocated that the biologists, instead of evolution, employ Darwin's own term - "descent with modification," in so far as progress is implied in the term evolution. Gould's suggestion has been largely ignored, though not by all scientists. The term evolution appears to be here to stay, though "descent with modification" continues to be employed by some scientists and others use another of Darwin's terms for evolution – "transformism," as Browne noted.[24]

Gould also opposed the concept of cultural progressive evolution and called it a "discredited theory" of ranking human groups and cultures. Gould proposed that "cultural change" be used in lieu of cultural evolution.[25]

Despite Darwin's cultural ranking from the lowest (the Fuegians) to the highest (the British), Browne stated, that he thought: "The possibility of change linked all mankind, according to circumstance, along the arc of culture." His acquaintance with the three Fuegians (especially Jemmy Button), convinced him that the gap could be closed, even in one generation. The three who had been "savages of the lowest type imaginable," had become "civilized Fuegians," within a very short time (while on board the *Beagle* and in England). His attitude was similar, in this respect, to that of the Anglican missionaries who worked on the premise that the Fuegians were savages, yet capable of being "saved," civilized and converted to Christianity... Now we return to the voyage.

CHAPTER 2

THE SECOND BEAGLE VOYAGE BEGINS: 1831-1832

1. PREPARATIONS FOR DEPARTURE: SEPTEMBER-DECEMBER 1831

The week after Fitz-Roy and Darwin first met (September 5) in London, they sailed to Plymouth to inspect the *Beagle*. Six weeks later, on October 24, Darwin returned in Devonport, the navy yard of Plymouth, ready to sail. He remained there and in Plymouth over two months, until the *Beagle* finally weighed anchor. Besides the "many & unexpected delays" his reiterated complaint was the lack of space on the *Beagle*. He would have to squeeze himself into a "private corner", hang his hammock over his table, to mention just two inconveniencies. However, the thought of seasickness may have worried him far more. On November 13, he made "a casual entry in his diary" that the three Fuegians had arrived accompanied by their schoolmaster and that the would-be-missionary, Matthews, had come at the same time.[26]

The three "protégés," having spent ten months in Walthamstow, bade farewell to their friends in October, and rode in a stagecoach back to London for the last time, accompanied by Mr. Jenkins, the schoolmaster. From there, they boarded a steam packet to Davenport with the heavy cargo of gifts that well-meaning churchgoers had inundated them. The seamen joked when they tried to fit it all into the small hold of the *Beagle*, especially the complete sets of crockery.[27] Darwin was appalled later, when he inspected the heaps of gifts.

> The choice of articles showed the most culpable folly & negligence. Wine-glasses, butter-bolts, tea-trays, soup turins, mahogany dressing case, fine white linen, beaver hats & an endless variety of similar things. The means absolutely wasted on such things would have purchased an immense stock of really useful articles.[28]

However inappropriate the gifts were, Jemmy, Fuegia and York highly valued each and every one. They well knew, or imagined, that things of this sort could be put to multiple uses. Jared Diamond, in his brilliant book *Guns, Germs, and Steel*, mentioned a somewhat similar situation while leaving camp with a group of native New Guineans. They played with his discarded objects "to figure out whether they might be useful." Some, such as discarded tin cans, posed no problem while others were "tested for purposes very different from the one for which they were manufactured."[29]

The date for departure was finally respected. On December 27, 1831, the *Beagle* sailed away with Fitz-Roy as commander and surveyor of the second expedition of "The Beagle's Circumnavigation of the Globe." Darwin didn't realize until later that the voyage was to last nearly five years.

2. THE CREW AND THE SUPERNUMERARIES

Captain Philip Parker King (the commander of the first *Beagle* and *Adventure* expedition: 1826-1830) came to see them off with his son, Philip Gidley King, who embarked on the *Beagle* as a midshipman. King the elder retired in 1834 and settled in Australia, where Darwin paid him a visit near the end of the voyage, in January 1836.[30] The entire group sailing on the *Beagle* totaled seventy-four; the crew plus nine passengers, called supernumeraries. Besides the captain, the crew was composed of the eleven officers and petty officers, a surgeon, his assistant, three midshipmen, eight marines, thirty-four seamen, and six boys. Only those who will become familiar as the narration continues will be mentioned here. Benjamin Bynoe, Jemmy's close friend during both voyages, was the assistant surgeon and later the "acting surgeon". Fitz-Roy was aware of Bynoe's fine qualities: his "affectionate kindness... his skill and attention...[that] will never be forgotten by any of his shipmates." Darwin also recalled Bynoe's "very kind attention to me when I was ill at Valparaíso " (in September 1834). Another midshipman, besides Philip King, was Robert Nicholas Hamond, Fitz-Roy's shipmate on the *Thetis* voyage (which lasted from 1824 to 1828), who joined the *Beagle* after departure, in Montevideo, and was known as "a very nice gentlemanlike person." Lieutenant John Clements Wickham was Fitz-Roy's special friend, had been on the first Beagle voyage, was now the second in command and proved to be a great help to Fitz-Roy during his moments of profound crisis. Darwin also esteemed him as "a glorious fellow" and "far the most conversible person on board." At thirty-three, he was the oldest officer. Lieutenant Bartholomew James Sulivan was Fitz-Roy's oldest friend on board. They had also been together on the *Thetis*. Fitz-Roy had requested that Sulivan be transferred to the *Beagle* when he had assumed command of her in October 1828. Young John Lort Stokes, the assistant surveyor, who had been on the first voyage, became Darwin's cabin mate and the officer whose company he seemed to prefer. James Bennett, Jemmy Button's other special friend. (along with Bynoe), had also been on the first *Beagle* expedition and had accompanied the Fuegians in England. He sailed on this voyage also, though Fitz-Roy failed to list him as a member of the crew, he did so later.[31] It is curious that Master Murray remained in England. He had assisted Fitz-Roy during the first voyage, chasing the whaleboat thieves and had discovered Beagle Channel in April 1830. Fitz-Roy seemed to esteem him highly.

One of the nine supernumeraries was Syms Covington, Darwin's servant, who often accompanied him on excursions on horseback in Uruguay, Argentina and Chile. Covington remained with Darwin as his secretary and servant until 1839 when he migrated to Australia. Another was Fitz-Roy's servant, seldom mentioned by name. George James Stebbing, the "instrument maker," though responsible for the twenty-four chronometers, was listed as a supernumerary. Augustus Earle, who was already a well-known artist, resigned from his post on the *Beagle* in August 1832 in Montevideo due to ill health. Like Darwin, he abhorred slavery. But Darwin and Fitz-Roy were "quite indignant" by

15

Earle's book, published in 1832, in which he severely criticized the missionaries he had met in New Zealand.[32] Conrad Martens replaced Earle in Montevideo. Darwin thought he had "rather too much of the drawing-master about him; he is very unlike to Earle's eccentric character." Earle was perhaps a more inspired artist than Martens, though the latter proved to be an extremely gifted landscape artist. Martens left the *Beagle* in Valparaíso late September 1834 and settled in Sydney where he continued drawing and remained in contact with Fitz-Roy.[33]

Attention should be called to the other five supernumeraries: Matthews, the trainee missionary; the newly civilized Fuegia Basket; her jealous suitor, York Minster; the fifteen or sixteen-year-old Jemmy Button, who was rarely seasick on the long voyages, though often homesick. The fifth, who would be seasick almost as frequently as homesick, was the twenty-two year old Charles Darwin, affectionately called Philos by Fitz-Roy and Flycatcher by the crew. He never ceased collecting flies, during the voyage, besides vast varieties of fish, birds, plants, rocks, shells, bones of contemporary quadruples and fossils of long extinct "bony giants." At least two of these fossils' "grandchildren" roam the arid steppes of Patagonia today: the humble armadillo and the huge rodent, capybara (water-hog). Darwin's eagerness to observe, inspect and collect seems insatiable. Although he sent Henslow numerous boxes and crates of specimens and rocks, he did not collect artifacts, much less human skeletons.[34] His collections, experiences, observations, and discoveries during this voyage would provide inspiration and some evidence to construct his theory *On the Origin of Species...* Here he proposed that all living forms were gradually transformed, through descent with modification, mainly by natural selection, from simple cell-like progenitors. We may have been "created" by a God out of a primordial chaos or have been the first-born of the original couple, Yoalox the younger and the beautiful Maku-kipa, as the Yamana believed. Be that as it may, we are part of a natural process of great antiquity, whose secrets are being unveiled by science. Browne explained:

> Every since returning from the Beagle voyage in 1836...he had believed that living beings were not created by divine fiat...He would become one of the most famous scientists of his day...not least for the manner in which he changed the way human beings thought about themselves and their

own place in nature...At his most determined, he questioned everything his contemporaries believed about living nature, calling forth a picture shorn of the Garden of Eden. No one could afterwards regard organic beings...with anything like the same eyes as before.[35]

3. WESTERN CIVILIZATION ARRIVES AT A CROSSROAD

One road leads to the divine origin of Man and all living creatures. It is pleasant to travel on, having many signposts and shrines along the way but it is circular: it ends up where it begins. The other road heads towards the natural origin of all species. It is difficult to follow, full of thorns, dead ends and detours but it leads to an infinite horizon.

Creation and Science respond to a search for the meaning of life. They are very dissimilar: one gives us solace while the other may be troubling but both are with us for an unknown future. Recall that Darwin became an agnostic: the door of his mind was open. Though he expressed no doubts about the validity of science, he emphasized the significance of religion in his later work, *The Descent of Man...* Yet it would unfair to Darwin for me to presume to penetrate his mind, beyond his written words.

Stephen Jay Gould commented: "Often, religion has actively encouraged science. If there is any consistent enemy of science, it is not religion, but irrationalism."[36]

Fitz-Roy had not reached his "spiritual destiny" during the voyage. His mind was also open. He offered Darwin the voyage (though Darwin's father paid his personal expenses), because he wanted a naturalist, a scientist, to accompany him. He also gave him the first volume of *Principles of Geology* by Charles Lyell who proved to be Darwin's greatest teacher. Almost all, if not all, Darwin scholars recognize that Lyell's geology was Darwin's initial inspiration in the vast field of natural science, that he applied Lyell's method of investigating and reasoning, and that he also went beyond him, as true disciples do.[37]

4. OFF TO TIERRA DEL FUEGO

The voyage to Tierra del Fuego took nearly a year (to December 17,1832), mainly because of many stopovers: Tenerife (one of the Canary islands), Cape Verde Islands, and along the east coast of South America: -Bahía, Río de Janeiro, Montevideo, Buenos Aires, Bahía Blanca and the mouth of Rio Negro (northern Patagonia, Argentina)- then down the coast to Tierra del Fuego. As early as September and October 1832, Darwin discovered important fossils (near Bahia Blanca, Argentina) and later, in 1833 and 1834, he made his extensive excursions on horseback while the *Beagle* crew was making surveys along the coasts of Uruguay and Argentina, or docked for repairs.[38]

5. DARWIN'S AND FITZ-ROY'S PORTRAITS OF THE THREE FUEGIANS: YORK, FUEGIA AND JEMMY

During the voyage to Tierra del Fuego Darwin had ample time to become acquainted with his three Fuegian shipmates. However he wrote so briefly about them in his diary during the voyage that Sandra Herbert suggested that he was not yet aware of "the extent of his own interest" in them.[39] He mentioned them frequently after the arrival in Tierra del Fuego. His only "portraits" of them, entirely quoted below, were apparently written shortly after the voyage. They were not recorded in his diary as Herbert noted.

> York Minster was a full-grown, short, thick, powerful man: his disposition was reserved, taciturn, morose, and when excited violently passionate; his affections were very strong towards a few friends on board; his intellect good.

> Fuegia Basket was a nice, modest, reserved young girl with a rather pleasing but sometimes sullen expression and very quick in learning anything, especially languages. This she showed in picking up some Portuguese and Spanish when left on shore for only a short time at Río de Janeiro and Monte Video, and in her knowledge of Eng-

3: York Minster in England: sketch by Fitz-Roy.

4: Fuegia Basket in England: by Fitz-Roy.

5: Jemmy Button with necktie in England: also by Fitz Roy.

lish. York Minster was very jealous of any attention paid to her; for it was clear he determined to marry her as soon as they were settled on shore.

Jemmy Button was a universal favourite, but likewise passionate; the expression of his face at once showed his nice disposition. He was merry, and often laughed and was remarkably sympathetic with anyone in pain: when the water was rough, I was often a little sea-sick, and he used to come to me and say in a plaintive voice, 'Poor, poor fellow!' but the notion, after his aquatic life, of a man being sea-sick, was too ludicrous, and he was generally obliged to turn on one side to hide a smile or laugh, and then he would repeat his "Poor, poor fellow!'.
He was of a patriotic disposition and he liked to praise his own tribe and country, in which he truly said there were 'plenty of trees,' and he abused all the other tribes: he stoutly declared that there was no Devil in his land.
Jemmy was short, thick and fat, but vain of his personal appearance; he used to wear gloves, his hair was neatly cut, and he was distressed if his well-polished shoes were dirtied. He was fond of admiring himself in a looking-glass.

And he concluded:

It seems yet wonderful to me, when I think over all his many good qualities, that he should have been of the same race, and doubtless partaken of the same character, with the miserable, degraded savages whom we first met here.[40]

Darwin recognized York´s and Fuegia's "good intellect". Note in the last paragraph that Jemmy was highly prased for his qualities, yet defiled for his character. Darwin also wrote that their mental faculties, were very similar "to ours," yet he made many and very debasing comments concerning their people. These contradictions were never resolved (see below chapter 3 and 6).

**6. Halimink, a Selk'nam, a so-called Oens-man, 1923: photograph by
Martin Gusinde.**

6. THE "OENS-MEN"

Many of the Selk'nam men (whom Jemmy called Oens-men) were six feet tall, while the Yamana men were rarely more than five and a half feet. The Selk'nam had large frames and were evenly developed, being great hikers and runners, never sitting all day in a canoe as the Yamana often did. When not hunting they wore long cloaks made of guanaco fur and donned a matching triangular headpiece that enhanced their figures.

Darwin's first view of these Oens-men occurred on December 17, 1832 while the *Beagle* was sailing beyond the Atlantic entrance to the Magellan Strait, down the coast of Tierra del Fuego, along the shore of Isla Grande. Fitz-Roy reported: "A group of Indians" standing on a high cliff, hailed the ship with smoke from a fire ignited for the purpose." From the distance, the crew and passengers could only distinguish tall men, with large dogs. While York and Jemmy were leaning over the deck peering at them, Jemmy suddenly shouted: "Oens-men-very bad men," telling the captain to fire on them. Fitz-Roy refused to comply. From now on Jemmy will often evoke the enmity between his "tribe" and these Oens-men.[41]

7. DARWIN'S FIRST EXPERIENCES WITH THE FUEGIANS IN GOOD SUCCESS BAY: DECEMBER 17-20, 1832

About noon on December 17, the *Beagle* turned the corner of the Isla Grande, at Cape San Diego, into the Strait of Le Maire, pushed on by a northerly wind amidst high breakers. As the ship veered into nearby Good Success Bay, the crew sighted "a group of Fuegians" (later known as Haush, mentioned above) on a summit at the entrance to the bay. They were eagerly shouting and waving skins beckoning the strangers to come ashore. Fitz-Roy ignored their greetings, so they quickly lit a fire, despite the downpour, and welcomed them again. He admired their ability to light a fire so rapidly in such a heavy rain, recalling the times he spent more than two hours struggling to do likewise.[42]

An astonished Darwin gazed at them,

partly concealed by the entangled forest, [they] were perched on a wild point overhanging the sea; and as we passed by, they sprang up and waving their tattered cloaks sent forth a loud and sonorous shout. The savages followed the ship, and just before dark we saw their fire, and again heard their wild cry.

That evening a gale and heavy squalls wiped across the bay from the surrounding mountains and the sea was even more tempestuous in the strait, outside of the bay. Darwin thought the name "Good Success Bay" appropriate. Appropriate though it was at the moment, in reality the bay was named for *Nuestra Señora del Buen Suceso* (*Our Lady of Good Success*), the ship of the Nodal expedition, the first European vessel to anchor there, in 1618.

8. THE MAIN ENCOUNTERS: DECEMBER 18

Fitz-Roy, Darwin, Matthews, Lieutenant Hamond and other officers "went to meet the Fuegians in their own land". These natives, the Haush, were not navigators; they were hunters, "foot people," like their neighbors the Oens-men, the Selk'nam.

One of the men "began to shout most vehemently" directing the strangers just where to pull ashore. When they landed, several men (the Haush) "looked rather alarmed, but continued talking and making gestures with great rapidity."[43] The women and children "had been sent away." Darwin was intrigued as he observed the four men.

It was without exception the most curious and interesting spectacle I ever beheld: I could not have believed how wide was the difference between savage and civilized man: it is greater than between a wild and domesticated animal, inasmuch as in man there is a greater power of improvement.

Their long cloaks of guanaco fur were thrown over one shoulder, leaving an arm exposed of the other "for any exercise they must be absolutely naked." The main "exercises" were pursuing the guanacos or

25

7. Good Success Bay. A painting by Alexander Buchan of a scene in January 1769 when Captain Cook and his men were camping there.

seals. Darwin noticed the "dirty coppery red colour" of the men's skin. Three were "powerful young men," painted with streaks of black powdered charcoal. The fourth, the oldest, apparently the chief, was distinguished by a bright red line from ear to ear, white lines above the eyelids and a headband of white feathers (an attribute of a shaman, rather than a chief). He thought they resembled the Patagonians (the Tehuelche Indians).

The Haush were remotely related to the Patagonians, and were physically very different from the Yamana, The Haush had migrated from the Patagonian mainland (now Argentina), perhaps thousands of years ago. The Selk'nam came later, though long before Magellan arrived, and eventually forced the Haush to take refuge in this extremity of the Isla Grande. The Selk'nam were warriors, men of action while the Haush were more peaceful and contemplative.[44]

The four men reminded Darwin of "the devils which come on the stage in plays like Der Freischutz." He was thinking of a "play" (an opera) he had seen in Edinburgh in 1824.[45]

Young Matthews, the would-be-missionary, thought that these Fuegians were "no worse than he had supposed them to be." In contrast to Darwin's and Matthews' dry comments, Lieutenant Hamond exclaimed: "What a pity such fine fellows should be left in such a barbarous state."

Though Darwin thought the men resembled devils, he also noticed that they appeared to be "distrustful, surprised and startled" and "abject." However, after receiving pieces red cloths, which they tied around their necks, "they became good friends." The "old man" welcomed each of his guests by patting their breasts and making a "chuckling kind of noise, as people do when feeding chickens." Then Darwin strolled down the beach with him "who demonstrated his good humour several times" by patting his breast again. He further reassured Darwin by three hard slaps simultaneously on his breast and back and "then bared his bosom for me to return the compliment, which being done, he seemed highly pleased." Following these cozy greetings, the linguistic barrier was erected. The Haush may have chatted with their guests hoping some meaning would seep through the barrier. If so, their efforts came to naught. Darwin remarked that their language (which he called Fuegian) "scarcely deserves to be called articulate," with its many "hoarse, guttural and clicking sounds."

The salutations over, the Haush attempted to amuse or impress their guests by mimicking their coughing and yawning and repeating "with perfect correctness each word in any sentence we addressed them, and they remembered such words for some time." Darwin also commented (or at least wrote): "Which of us, for instance, could follow an American Indian through a sentence of more than three words?" This comment would have pleased the Haush.

Darwin surmised that their talent for mimicry was common to all savages, such as the "Caffirs" (of South Africa, now a derogatory term) and the native Australians. He wondered if this could be explained by the greater practice of perception and the keener senses of people in "a savage state as compared with those long civilized."[46]

That evening (still day light) after dinner on the ship, they returned with York and Jemmy, who apparently came for the first time. Soon after landing, several of the officers squinted and made monkey-faces to amuse their hosts. Thereupon one of the young Haush, his face painted black with white bands over the eyes, mimicked their "monkey-faces" making "still more hideous grimaces." About then a sailor began singing and dancing a waltz. Darwin with the others joined in the fun and he later commented: "When a song was struck up, I though they would have fallen down with astonishment; & with equal delight they viewed our dancing and immediately began themselves to waltz with one of the officers."

After waltzing on the beach for a while, one of young natives motioned to compare his height and his good looks with a "chosen opponent," the tallest of the *Beagle* crew. The two men stood back to back, as the former tried to find higher ground and stand on tiptoe. Darwin was observing him closely.

> He opened his mouth to show his teeth, and turned his face for a side view; and all this was done with such alacrity, that I dare say he thought himself the handsomest man in Tierra del Fuego. After our first feeling of grave astonishment was over, nothing could be more ludicrous than the odd mixture of surprise and imitation which these savages every moment exhibited.

Fitz-Roy also found them good-humored though he objected when they offered to test their strength by wrestling with one or two sailors. He refused to allow competition of this sort between his men and the Haush nor did he permit wrestling later with the Yamana men. He had learned. from reading the sealer James Weddell's book (published in 1827), that one of Weddell's sailors had lost a wrestling match with a young Yamana. Fitz-Roy didn't want to risk such a humiliation.

Skin color was another matter. The Haush compared theirs with that of some of the sailors, expressing "the liveliest surprise and admiration at its whiteness, just in the same way in which I have seen the orangutan do at the Zoological Gardens." Darwin was very fond of orangutans though, as far as I recall from reading him, he never compared Englishmen to orangutans.

In a more serious vein he noticed: "They knew what guns were & much dreaded them, & nothing would tempt them to take one in their hands." They asked for knives, using the Spanish word as *cuchilla* (*cuchillo*). To make sure they were understood, the men pretended to hold a piece of meat in their mouths while making gestures of slicing it.

The old man "addressed a long harangue to Jemmy, which it seems was to invite him to stay with them." Darwin clarified that "Jemmy understood very little of their language, and was, moreover, thoroughly ashamed of his countrymen." Fitz-Roy thought that: "It was amusing and interesting to see their meeting with York and Jemmy, who would not acknowledge them as countrymen, but laughed at and mocked them." He observed that even though York didn't understand their language, he suddenly burst out laughing at something the old man said to him. York couldn't resist telling everyone that the old man had said that "he was dirty and to pull out his beard." Fitz-Roy deduced that if the language the old man spoke really differed as much as they pretended, York could not have understood the old man. However, Darwin noticed that the natives realized immediately that York and Jemmy were from Tierra del Fuego and that they understood a little of their language. But he wondered why the old man had admonished York to pull out the twenty hairs of his "beard," while the "untrimmed" beards of the crew failed to incite any comment from the old man. I might add here that the Fuegians considered eyebrows and all face hair repulsive (of course except eyelashes) so York easily interpreted the old man's reproach.[47]

For Fitz-Roy it was "painful" to contemplate such savages as "even remotely descended from human beings." It was painful because he could not help thinking of his own ancestors, the Britons, whom Caesar had seen "painted and clothed in skins, like these Fuegians." They reminded him of children, like his ancestors, the latter having gradually grown into civilized Englishmen.

9. THE LAST BRIEF ENCOUNTERS: DECEMBER 19 AND 20

The same (four) men appeared "with their timid children," on December 19. Otherwise Darwin did not mention the children, or any encounters that day. His last entry, on December 20, was also very brief. The same four Haush men had returned to the beach "with a reinforcement of natives who most likely came to beg for 'Cochillas' [knives]."[48]

10. DARWIN RECALLS HIS FIRST IMPRESSIONS OF THE FUEGIANS

He wrote to Professor Henslow in April, 1833:

The Fuegians [the Haush] are in a more miserable state of barbarism than I had expected ever to have seen a human being...I do not think any spectacle can be more interesting, than the first sight of Man in his primitive wildness...I shall never forget, when entering Good Success Bay, the yell with which a party received us. They were seated on a rocky point, surrounded by the dark forest of beech; as they threw their arms wildly round their heads & their long hair streaming they seemed the troubled spirits of another world.[49]

And to his sister Caroline, also April 1833:

No drawing or description will at all explain the extreme interest which is created by the first sight of savages. It is an interest which almost repays one for a cruize in these latitudes: & this I assure you is saying a good deal.[50]

The next month, in a letter to his cousin William Darwin Fox, he mentioned the Fuegians (the Haush of Good Success Bay) "In Tierra del Fuego I saw bona fide savages; & they are as savage as the most curious person would desire. A wild man is indeed a miserable animal, but one well worth seeing."[51] Again he was thinking of the Good Success natives when he wrote to a friend, a year and seven months later in July 1834.

> I have seen nothing which more completely astonished me, than the first sight of a Savage; It was a naked Fuegian his long hair blowing about, his face besmeared with paint. There is in their countenances, an expression, which I believe to those who have not seen it, must be inconceivably wild. Standing on a rock he uttered tones & made gesticulations than which, the crys of domestic animals are far more intelligible.[52]

The last pages of *The Voyage...*

> One's mind hurries back over past centuries, and then asks, could our progenitors have been men like these? - men, whose very signs and expressions are less intelligible to us than those of the domesticated animals; men, who do not possess the instinct of those animals, nor yet appear to boast of human reason, or at least of arts consequent on that reason.
> I do not believe it is possible to describe or paint the difference between savage and civilised man. It is the difference between a wild and tame animal.[53]

On the final pages of *The Descent of Man...*(1871) Darwin evoked the Fuegians (the Haush) again in this often-quoted passage:

> The main conclusion arrived at in this work, namely, that man is descended from some lowly organised form, will, I

regret to think, be highly distasteful to many. But there can hardly be a doubt that we are descended from barbarians. The astonishment which I felt on first seeing a party of Fuegians on a wild and broken shore will never be forgotten by me, for the reflection at once rushed into my mind-such were our ancestors...[54]

By 1876, when his life's work had taken form, in his autobiographic notes he wrote with nostalgia:

I remember when in Good Success Bay, in Tierra del Fuego, thinking (and I believe that I wrote home to the effect) that I could not employ my life better than in adding a little to natural science. This I have done to the best of my abilities, and critics may say what they like, but they cannot destroy this conviction.[55]

There can no doubt that this meeting with the Haush had a lasting effect on Darwin's concept of the "savage." Though he mocked them, his recollections of them were more of astonishment than derision, in stark contrast to his later impressions of other "Fuegians," (the Yamana) near Cape Horn.

11. IMAGINE FOR A MOMENT

One of the Haush men might have told his wife (or wives) and children about these encounters in Good Success Bay (with this fictitious quote). "I was surprised when I first spotted their enormous canoe with three huge sails coming towards us into the bay. The men came ashore the next day, all rather young. I was surprised but I wasn't amazed because we've seen such canoes [ships] and men like them before, with disgusting hair all over their faces, no paint at all, and such colorless skin. They were all wrapped up, even their heads, and wore the largest, longest sandals [boots] I've ever seen, as if they couldn't resist a little cold. Such a load of clothes they couldn't run if they tried. But they were friendly and droll, laughing at our mimicry, and singing and dancing to please us. It was jolly. We all had fun, especially when I think of those the not-so-funny sealers roaming around the strait destroying our food supply."[56]

12. DARWIN'S "GOOD SUCCESS EXCURSIONS": DECEMBER 19 AND 20

The 19th Darwin and several companions penetrated inland, pushing and crawling through the thick forest, climbing over decaying trees and "putrefying vegetable matter," while treading lightly over the peat bogs. They hiked up the hills along the rocky banks of the streams and down steep valleys. It was easier climbing a mountainside "where a great slip had cleared a straight space." (I saw such cleared spaces while there in 1970). Arriving at a summit, Darwin felt "amply repaid by the grandeur of the scene," though it depressed him. "Death, instead of Life, seemed the predominate spirit."[57]

Darwin and others ventured a bit farther inland on the fourth, the last full day in Good Success Bay, December 20. On the way, they recalled the misadventure of Captain Cook's first voyage in 1769 when Sir Joseph Banks, the aristocratic botanist, explored the same hinterland with two servants who died there of exposure during a snow storm in the mid-summer of January. Darwin and his party, who were there in the same season, were more fortunate. They reached the summit of the highest mountain flanking the bay, Mount Banks, which Darwin did not mention by name, though Fitz-Roy did. Towards the south (towards Montes Negros) they came upon,

> a scene of savage magnificence, well becoming Tierra del Fuego. There was a degree of mysterious grandeur in the mountain behind mountain, with the deep intervening valleys, all covered by one thick, dusky mass of forest. The atmosphere, likewise, in this climate, where gale succeeds gale, with rain, hail, and sleet, seems blacker than anywhere else.[58]

Darwin collected plants and sighted one or two guanacos though he missed his shots. He greatly admired these guanacos even though he attempted to kill them.

8. Guanacos then and now, thanks are due to the Chilean photographer Alan Warren.

These beautiful animals are truly alpine in their habits, & in their wildness well come the surrounding landscape. I cannot imagine anything more graceful than their action: they start on a canter & when passing through rough ground they dash like a thorough bred hunter. The noise they make is very peculiar & somewhat resemble the neighing of a colt.[59]

13. ON TOWARDS CAPE HORN: CHRISTMAS AND THE LAST WEEK OF 1832

Fitz-Roy headed the *Beagle* towards Cape Horn, early the next day, December 21. Darwin noted in his diary that the sea and atmosphere were so calm that it would surprise those "who think that in this the region winds & waters never cease fighting." Sure enough, the very next night Cape Horn "demanded its tribute and sent us a gale right in our teeth."[60]

Christmas eve was passed in a high sea: squalls and hail descended with such violence that the *Beagle* took refuge on Hermite Island, in Saint Martin's Cove (that Darwin invariably called Wigwam Cove, which he confused with the name of a cove nearby). Saint Martin's Cove had become the favorite Cape Horn refuge for English sealers and explorers.

James Weddell and his assistant mate, Mathew Brisbane, had been there in November 1823 in their small vessels the *Jane* and the *Beaufoy*. Captain Henry Foster, in the *Chanticleer* and Captain Philip Parker King, in the *Adventure*, spent weeks there in March and April 1829, as Fitz-Roy had on the *Beagle*, in April 1830.

Despite the heavy gale and rough seas, Christmas day was merry in this "snug little harbour." After breakfast Darwin, Sulivan, and Hamond climbed Kater's Peak (1700 feet) that overlooks the bay. They were rewarded with a magnificent view of the islands that are formed of mountaintops, where the Cordillera of the Andes almost sinks into the sea, at Cape Horn. "Whilst looking round on this inhospitable region, we could scarcely credit that man existed on it." Sulivan was amused by rolling down huge rocks from the summit while Darwin hammered others with his geological tools (for specimens). They and Hamond screamed repeatedly to hear their echoes and fired their guns at the birds in caverns nearby.

When they returned to the *Beagle*, they were told that they had been seen from the ship, crawling over the rocks. They were puzzled when they realized it had been impossible to see them because the *Beagle* was anchored under a nearby cliff that blocked the view of Kater's peak. Darwin surmised that the men they saw crawling over some rocks were Fuegians (Yamanas). The local Yamana had certainly heard the racket of shouts, tumbling rocks and gunfire that Darwin and the others had made. "They must have thought us the powers of darkness; or whatever else, fear has kept them concealed." This may be why they didn't appear at all during the week the *Beagle* was there, because they had welcomed the previous British ships.

That midnight, violent squalls funneled down through the surrounding hills striking the water in the cove. Snow, hail, and rain soon followed, all this in early summer. During six long days and nights "three anchors down and plenty of chain cable out," steadied the ship. Neither Fitz-Roy nor Darwin account for these days except for lamenting the "wretched climate," and briefly mentioning visits to nearby bays and islands from December 27 to 29, though without seeing any natives there either.[61]

CHAPTER 3

DARWIN'S "MEDITATIONS" (MY TERM)
ABOUT THE FUEGIANS

His "meditations" (my term) on the Fuegians (the Yahgans) read, in chapter ten of *The Voyage of the Beagle*, as if he had penned them when he and the others were obliged to remain in and near "Wigwam Cove" (Saint Martin's Cove) due to the "very bad weather," this last week of 1832. He deliberately grouped most of his diary notes on Tierra del Fuego in this one chapter, without dating them. See this note for my rather detailed explanation of his "meditations" sources.[62] I have also used Darwin's *The Descent of Man...* and *On the Origin of Species...* Citations of other authors appear under the headings of "meditations" with the intention of presenting a brief view of the Yamana mode of living. Some authors have quoted or paraphrased Darwin's texts to characterize the Fuegians, though he probably had no idea he would be used as an authority on them.

He began by explaining that every bay in the neighborhood (of Saint Martin's Cove) might be called Wigwam Cove "with equal propriety," in the sense that in nearly all the bays they visited, or saw in passing, there was evidence that the Indians had inhabited them. The French archaeologist, Dominique Legoupil, published the earliest date recorded so far in the Cape Horn archipelago: approximately 580 A.D. (from an excavation on Bayly Island). Even though she and her team located and dated over thirty sites in the area, it is possible that earlier dates may be found there.[63]

9. "A canoe with Yahgans of Wollaston Island": drawing by Conrad Martens.

1. THE WOLLASTON ISLANDERS
"THE MOST ABJECT AND MISERABLE CREATURES..."

Darwin was especially observant of the Yamana-Yahgans he saw along the coast of Wollaston Island, near Cape Horn. This long quotation concerns them.

> While going one day [25 February 1834] on shore near Wollaston Island, we pulled along side a canoe with six Fuegians. These were the most abject and miserable creatures I anywhere beheld... [They] were quite naked, and even one full-grown woman was absolutely so. It was raining heavily, and the fresh water, together with the spray, trickled down her body.
>
> In another harbour not far distant a woman who was suckling a recently-born child came one day alongside the vessel, and remained there out of mere curiosity, whilst the sleet fell and thawed on her naked bosom and on the skin of her naked baby!
>
> These poor wretches were stunted in their growth, they're hideous faces bedaubed with white paint, their skins filthy and greasy, their hair entangled, their voices discordant and their gestures violent. Viewing such men, one can hardly make oneself believe that they are fellow creatures and inhabitants of the same world.
>
> It is a common subject of conjecture what pleasure in life some of the lower animals can enjoy: how much more reasonably the same question may be asked with respect to these barbarians! At night five or six human beings, naked and scarcely protected from the wind and rain of this tempestuous climate sleep on the wet ground coiled up like animals.

He painted a devastating picture of these Wollaston Islanders "the most abject and miserable creatures," paddling from place to place, camping along these bleak shores in cloudy atmosphere that made the region seem worst that it really was. He lacked compassion for these people. I question his impressions of them also when he failed to comment on the scenes he witnessed. If their voices were "discordant" and their gestures "violent," were they trying to communicate something urgent to the strangers? Did he actually see them sleeping "on wet ground coiled up like animals"? Or did someone tell him they did? Nor did he ask himself why they had such "filthy and greasy" skins. George Stocking Jr considered these comments "a kind of hurried, unanalysed ethnographic gestalt, in which paint and grease and body structure blended into a single perception of physical type..."[64]

2. THEIR HUT, A "HAYCOCK"

Darwin thought their hut was like a "haycock" because it "consists of a few broken branches stuck in the ground, and very imperfectly thatched on one side with a few tufts of grass and rushes. The whole cannot be the work of an hour and it is only used for a few days."[65] Here he explained why they were so "imperfectly thatched." However, not all Yamana "haycocks" were like these. According to Carlos Spegazzini: "Their hemispheric form have such perfect curves, that one wonders how they were able to obtain them with such coarse materials."[66] The latter quote it not meant to counter Darwin but simply to point out that the Yahgans constructed similar huts in a more perfected form.

3. THEIR FIRE

Darwin stated that the "discovery" of fire, was "probably the greatest event made by man, except for language, and dates from before the dawn of history." Although he didn't mention fire in his "meditations," he did in *The Descent of Man*...[67] His awareness of its vital importance justifies its insertion here. Almost all the reports on the Fuegians' use of fire emphasize their efforts to keep it burning as long as possible. The Yamana kept fires in their canoes at all times, when possible. There was little danger that the canoe burn up because the fire was placed on a support of mud and sand, was constantly supervised, and the canoe was humid. Fitz-Roy insisted that though the Yamana keep the fire alive nearly at all times, "they are at no loss to rekindle it...With two stones (usually iron pyrites) they procure a spark."[68]

10. A Yamana man, wearing the "couple" for lighting fire; painting by Eduardo Armstrong, based on a photograph.

One stone had to be pyrite. The other could be a hard stone such as flint (silex), later a nail, an axe head or any small iron object. But why is pyrite so effective? The brief answer is because of the sulfuric gases it contains.[69]

These two stones formed a couple, a *matuku*: the pyrite was the husband *wa* and the flint, his wife *kipa*. The men carried this couple wherever they went, usually wrapped in a small leather bag, which they hung from their neck. The Alakaluf, Selk'nam and Haush did likewise.[70]

The only known iron pyrite source for the Yamana was in Mercury Sound on Captain Arcane Island along the Cockburn Channel in Alakaluf territory. Lucas Bridges visited the site and described it as follows:

> In a snug harbour a well-worn trail led to a large deposit of refuse, evidence that the natives had worked there for centuries. The heaps of chippings were huge, and to this day there are to be seen the rounded masses of iron pyrites from which, with great labour, both Yahgan and Alacaloof obtained their supplies. Those of the islanders who could not reach Mercury Sound would give handsome presents in exchange for the firestone, rather than use the much-inferior flints available in their own localities.[71]

Although Mercury Sound was deep into Alakaluf territory, the Yamana may have had access to it. In any event they could obtain pyrite from these neighbors by barter.

The tinder of course had to be a very dry inflammable material: duvet, bird's down, was often used, as well as ground fungus, splinters, and in an emergency dry insects' nests or dry grass, and so forth.

4. THEY LIVED "CHIEFLY ON SHELLFISH..."

Darwin surmised that the Fuegians (near Saint Martin's Cove) lived,

> chiefly upon shell-fish, [and] are obliged constantly to change their place of residence: but they return at intervals to the same spots, as is evident from the piles of old shells, which must often amount to many tons in weight.

These heaps can be distinguished at a long distance by the bright green colour of certain plants, which invariably grow on them.[72]

He had the erroneous impression that these Yamanas relied chiefly on shellfish and fish.

Whenever it is low water, winter or summer, night or day, they must rise to pick shell-fish from the rocks; and the women either dive to collect sea-eggs, or sit patiently in their canoes, and with a baited hairline without any hook, jerk out little fish. If a seal is killed, or the floating carcass of a putrid whale discovered, it is a feast; and such miserable food is assisted by a few tasteless berries and fungi.[73]

He had no way of knowing then (In 1832 or later), that the populations of seals and whales had been greatly reduced by the English and Yankee "big time fishermen" who had worked around Cape Horn and the outer reaches of the Antarctic from the late eighteenth century to about 1829.

Here I quote from chapter 2 of my unpublished text, mentioned in the above Acknowledgements.

When Edmund Fanning, a native of Connecticut, an active sealer, stopped over in the vicinity of Cape Horn, In September of 1817, while heading for the South Seas, he and his crew found fur seals, highly coveted for "their thick coat and fine cast of a reddish hue." He did not say if any remained. Near Cape Horn, in Nassau Bay, he came upon vast numbers of the prized right whales. Soon afterwards these top quality seals and whales undoubtedly continued to be "harvested" there by Fanning's other ships and those of his competitors.

The Yahgans were certainly aware of the Yankee ships sailing through their territory, of the boat-loads of whalers harpooning in their bays and channels, of sealers busy killing on their rookeries, and of the vessels wrecked in their dangerous waters.[74]

Fitz-Roy was less disparaging about the Indian women fishing than Darwin. He noted that the crew learned from them and could catch several dozen in a few hours. Darwin was also mistaken when he stated that the natives did not use wild celery and scurvy grass.[75] Celery was eaten occasionally and the tough grass served as bedding, and lining sandals. But recall that Darwin did not presume to be making "scientific" statements; he wrote his impressions of the Fuegians, gathered from his own observations and what he had heard about them,

Whale meat was essential when starvation threatened, as Darwin learned later from the sealer, William Low. Darwin described the scene, that Low had told him about having witnessed of a group Chono Indians, north of the Magellan Strait who were nearly starving because a succession of gales had prevented the women from collecting shellfish.[76] Darwin was probably correct in assuming that the Chonos were very like the Fuegians in this respect. He quoted Low's account of a party of Chonos returning from a four days' journey in search of food "excessively tired, each man carrying a great square piece of putrid whale-blubber with a hole in the middle, through which they put their heads, like the Gauchos do through their ponchos or cloaks."

"An old man cut off thin slices [of the blubber]....muttering over them." They roasted the slices for a minute and "distributed them to the famished party who during this time preserved a profound silence." Low also observed the Chonos burying large pieces of the whale meat in the sand, for future use.[77]

The Yahgans took advantage of stranded whales, even when they were not starving. Whale meat was much appreciated but it was not a primary food, such as the meat of seals, because the Yamana were not equipped to hunt healthy whales. They did attack dying whales with their harpoons to hasten their demise. However, they mainly sought whales that became stranded along the coasts. Stranding happened quite frequently when whales were still abundant. They were often attacked by orcas, the so-called killer whales. As the orcas only ate their tongues, the whales were left to die a lingering death and eventually either sank, were washed on shore or occasionally were killed off by the Yamana.

However, they had more reliable and varied "gifts of nature:" vast schools or shoals of sprats, a small fish that appeared in certain known

11. Titled: "Una Fiesta Fueguina." Scene of a beached whale; drawing by Giacomo Bove, 1883.

places in the autumn. Then the men would be kept busy fishing with nets. Lucas Bridges explained that these great quantities of sprats also attracted "seals, penguins, mollymauks and other sea-birds, and deep-water fish." This was a time of superabundance of prey for the natives and might last two months.[78]

None of the Tierra del Fuego natives were equipped to store suffi-cient food to live through prolonged periods of scarcity. Hardships and famines occurred, mainly due to the unpredictable and often harsh cli-mate.

5. "THEY KILL AND DEVOUR THEIR OLD WOMEN..."

Darwin was utterly indignant by the stories about the Fuegians (Yamanas) cannibalistic habits, that he heard mostly from the sealer Low and Fitz-Roy. Jemmy and York had told the latter, in 1830 on the way back to England during the first *Beagle* voyage, (mostly by ges-tures) that their people "made a practice of eating their enemies taken in war." More precisely, that the women ate the arms and the men the legs while the trunk and head were thrown into the sea. "A still more revolting account was given... respecting the horrible fate of the eldest women of their own tribes, when there is an unusual scarcity of food." Fitz-Roy thought at first that these accounts amounted to a "misunder-stood story." But they repeated them so often, as they learned to express themselves more fluently in English, until finally Fitz-Roy declared: "I no longer hesitate to state my firm belief in the most debas-ing trait of their character which will be found in these pages."[79] Low, the Scottish sealer quoted above, whom Fitz-Roy met during this sec-ond voyage, affirmed that they were indeed cannibals. Darwin cited Low's "native boy" Bob, a native Chono, in this often quoted text:

> The different tribes when at war are cannibals. From the concurrent but quite independent evidence of the boy taken by Mr. Low, and of Jemmy Button, it is certainly true, that when pressed in winter by hunger, they kill and devour their old women before they kill their dogs: the boy, being asked by Mr. Low why they did this, answered, 'Doggies catch otters, old women no'. The boy described

the manner in which they are killed by being held over smoke and thus choked; he imitated their screams *as a joke*, and described the parts of their bodies, which are considered best to eat.

Horrid as such a death by the hands of their friends and relatives must be, the fears of the old women, when hunger begins to press, are more painful to think of; we were told that they then often run away into the mountains, but that they are pursued by the men and brought back to the slaughter house at their own fire-sides![80]

As revealed in the above text, Bob was joking when he told the tale of the old women screaming but Darwin was horrified. He expressed utter indignation in a letter to his sister Caroline in March 1833.

These Fuegians are Cannibals; but we have good reason to suppose it carried on to an extent which hitherto has been unheard of in the world...Was ever anything so atrocious heard of, to work them [the old women] like slaves to procure food in the summer & occasionally in winter to eat them... I feel quite a disgust at the very sound of the voices of these miserable savages.[81]

A few months after he arrived home (in 1836), while having tea with Henslow and Joseph Romilly, a "fellow" at Trinity College, he informed them,

that in 'terra el fuego' whenever a scarcity occurs (wch [sic] is every 5 or 6 years) they kill the old women as the most useless living creatures; in conseq. [sic] when a famine beings the old women run away into the woods & many of them perish miserably.[82]

Even in his great work of 1859 he recalled: "We see the value set on animals even by the barbarians of Tierra del Fuego, by their killing and devouring their old women, in times of dearth, as of less value than their dogs."[83]

47

It is truly amazing that Darwin regarded Jemmy, Fitz-Roy's informant on cannibalism, as a reliable source, because he stated that it was "singularly difficult to obtain much information from them [Jemmy and York], concerning the habits of their countrymen". Also, "it was generally impossible to find out, by cross-questioning, whether one had rightly understood anything which they had asserted." Moreover, he knew that Bob, Low's Chono informant on cannibalism, was "called a liar, which in truth he was."[84]

Darwin had reasons to doubt the veracity of Bob's and Jemmy's stories but he didn't. The vision of old women being devoured was too powerful for him to resist. Moreover, cannibalism was expected among a people at such a "low level" of humanity, and this may also explain why he was so credulous.

Definitive refutation of cannibalism among the Yamana came from Thomas Bridges' son Lucas, who knew the Yahgan since his birth. He explained how Fitz-Roy and Darwin were misled.

> We [Lucas and his siblings] who later passed many years of our lives in daily contact with these people can find only one explanation for this shocking mistake [Darwin's conviction that the Fuegians were cannibals]. We suppose that, when questioned, York Minster, or Jimmy Button, would not trouble in the least to answer truthfully, but would merely give the reply that he felt was expected or desired. In the early days their limited knowledge of English would not allow them to explain at any length, and, as we know, it is much easier to answer "yes" than "no." So the statements with which these young men and little Fuegia Basket have been credited were, in fact, no more than agreement with suggestions made by their questioners.[85]

Leonard Engel, the editor of the 1962 edition of *The Voyage...* corrected Darwin's erroneous statements concerning the old women.

> Unfortunately, both Darwin and Fitz Roy were misled on the point, for the Fuegians were not cannibals and honoured rather than ate their old women. Old women were in demand as second and third wives...because of their

48

experience in the management of canoes and many duties performed by the Fuegian wife. A form of euthanasia by strangulation was practiced but this was confined to the incurably sick and disabled.[86]

Darwin had not read about the Yamana being accused of eating twelve Dutch sailors when they first met Europeans in 1624, near Cape Horn. Apparently the accusation was true but this incident, the only one on cannibalism that is documented, does not make the Yamana cannibals forever before and ever after. Cannibalism has occurred in dire circumstances, probably from "time immemorial": in situations of panic (as apparently in 1624), of starving survivors of shipwrecks and more recently of airplane crashes. When cannibalism is an integral part of a culture, as among the Aztecs, it is almost invariably ritualized. But is cannibalism a cardinal sin? Darwin thought so. The vision of these cannibals consuming their old women was too much for him: these people were "miserable savages," nothing could redeem them, even though Jemmy had made the leap to civilization and despite his friendly relations with him and other Yamanas, as will be noted below.

6. THEIR LANGUAGE
(ANOTHER SERIOUS MISTAKE DARWIN MADE)

Darwin's accusation of cannibalism reminded Lucas Bridges of another serious mistake Darwin made.

> The belief that the Fuegians were cannibals was not the only mistake Charles Darwin made about them. Listening to their speech, he got the impression that they were repeating the same phrases over and over again, and therefore came to the conclusion that something like one hundred words would cover the whole language. We who learned as children to speak Yahgan knew that, within its own limitation, it is infinitely richer and more expressive than English or Spanish. My father's Yahgan (or Yamana) English Dictionary... contains no fewer than 32,000 words and inflections, the number

of which might have been greatly increased without departing from correct speech.[87]

Lucas' statement seems to me conclusive.

7. "WHEN AT WAR [THEY] ARE CANNIBALS..."

Darwin asserted that: "The different tribes when at war are cannibals," and that each tribe,

> Is surrounded by other hostile tribes speaking different
> dialects, and separated from each other only by a desert-
> ed border or neutral territory: the cause of their warfare
> appears to be the means of subsistence.[88]

Here Darwin exaggerated. Only two "tribes" were separated by a no-
man's land, a zone along Beagle Channel. Fitz-Roy was less emphatic:
"Warfare, though nearly continual, is so desultory, and on so small a
scale among them, that the restraint and direction of their elders,
advised as they are by the doctors [shamans], is sufficient."[89]

Two top-ranking socio-biologists at Harvard University, Charles J.
Lumsden and Edward O. Wilson, were "intrigued" by warfare among
the hunter-gatherers, notably by Darwin's Fuegians.

> Some extraordinary set of circumstances –the prime
> movers of the origin of mind – must have existed to bring
> the early hominids across the Rubicon and into the irre-
> versible march of cultural evolution... One of the most
> intriguing explanations, suggested by Charles Darwin him-
> self, is warfare. There is plenty of evidence of violent
> aggression among recent bands of hunter-gatherers,
> whose social organization most closely resembles that of
> primitive man.

However, these professors had second thoughts on warfare during
the "march of cultural evolution." Three pages later they affirmed: "The

driving force then propelling the human species from the *Homo habilis* to the *Homo sapiens* level was not war, sex, climate or hunting on the savanna but gene-culture coevolution."[90] What a relief: neither we nor the Yahgans can be held responsible for past and present warfares.

Combats were not motivated to acquire "means of subsistence," much less to make a meal of an enemy. Some could result in the death of one or several of the male participants and women being kidnapped ("stolen"). She could be forced to become a wife, or one of the wives, of the enemy. Many were motivated by vengeance for a murder, a death attributed to a shaman's "magic," mistreatment of a woman by her husband, and for plunder. The latter motive became dominant when the *Beagle's* whaleboat with all of its equipment was stolen in February 1830 and a serious fight took place when an Alakaluf was killed by one of Fitz-Roy's crew. As will be seen in the next chapter, supplies from the *Beagle* motivated several attacks on Jemmy's tribe. Plunder for "imported goods" also incited an attack against the Anglican missionary ship in 1858 that culminated in the massacre of 1859, in Wulaia, the only massacre following that of 1624. In 1859, Jemmy's youngest brother killed the Anglican missionary, with the help of others. Seven members of his crew were stoned to death apparently by the invading Ones-men with the complicity of some local Yamana. One member of the crew, the cook, escaped, later returned to Wulaia, was treated kindly by the women, survived unharmed and became one of the principle witnesses for the British authorities in the Falklands (Malvinas). Plunder occurred then also but apparently the main objective was to drive the missionaries away, to prevent them from settling in their land. These two massacres are only reported aggressions against the whites during more than four centuries of contact. Massacres on this scale among the Fuegians themselves are unknown.

According to Gusinde, the women were crueler while fighting than the men, though they didn't use weapons or kill anyone. In the heat of a quarrel they would bite one another, strike the mouth or nose with a hard blow and tug each other's hair without mercy. When the Yamana fought on the water, the women paddlers closed in on their enemy's canoe while the men attacked one another with spears. To avoid a combat or following one, an avenging-aggressive party might accept gifts as compensation. Hyades insisted that there were never expeditions for war among the Yahgans but that they were very "touchy" (*susceptibles*) and inclined to quarrel or fight. Those present during a fight between two men might endeavor to calm them, take their weapons and forcibly separate them. Hyades cited Thomas Bridges' statement that only two murders occurred each year during thirteen years (from 1871 to 1884), which Hyades found surprisingly few.[91] Though the Yamana were apparently prone to quarrel and did attack neighbors, they were not trained as warriors.

8. BURIALS IN CAVES AND FORESTS

Darwin thought that the Fuegians buried their dead in caves "and sometimes in the mountain forests," which is true enough. Sometimes they interred the corpse in the ground near the camp where the person died or incinerated it on a pile of wood or dry bushes. The property of the deceased was usually destroyed by fire or buried with the corpse, except the dogs. The missionaries endeavored to put a stop to these customs and to persuade them to bury their dead in cemeteries. The Fuegians did not worship their ancestors. They even avoided approaching the place where a family member had died. Nor did they name the deceased. Such disregard for the dead is more apparent than real. A mourning ceremony for an adult family member or shaman might last off and on for months. On such occasions they carefully painted a variety of designs on their faces with carbon from the camp fires, fasted, and inflected serious wounds on themselves while chanting hour upon hour, day after day.

Mourning for the very young did not require a long ceremony. When an infant or child died the parents and other mourners shouted curses, screamed expressing their fury, against the "supreme deity," Watawineiwa, according to Gusinde, for taking the life of such an innocent creature. When a person had been assassinated, sooner or later the relatives would attempt to avenge the murder, as mentioned above. Often a hostile shaman would be blamed for the death of loved one. A mock battle might be performed to honor someone who had been murdered or even had died "normally" of old age, of a wound or by drowning. Two groups would be formed, one of men with clubs, another of women with especially painted long sticks or simply their canoe paddles. They

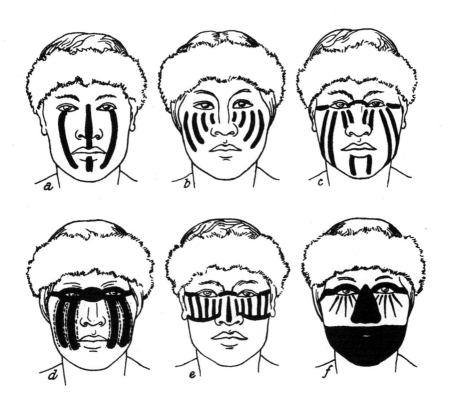

12. "Designs for the paint for mourning;" Gusinde 1986: vol. 3, 1102.

would simulate a fight by gestures of beating each other (of the same sex), and some could get hurt. Apparently they also argued and gestured in pairs of the same sex. One individual would be a relative or a friend of the deceased while the other might be the proven murderer. In the latter case he (almost invariably a man) would be thoroughly beaten, though apparently not killed. If a murder was not involved, the two would defy and blame each other for not haven taken better care of deceased, while praising his or her qualities. The other participants, the "audience," urged them on, chanting the laments. When alcohol was ruining their lives, in 1907, an American, Charles W. Furlong, happened to witness such a mock battle, that by then had became a drunken brawl.[92]

9. NO RELIGION

Darwin thought that they did not "perform any sort of religious worship." The nearest approach to "a religious feeling" that he had heard about was the manner in which York reacted to Bynoe during the first voyage back to England (in 1830). York had warned Bynoe that "much rain, snow, blow much" would come as punishment for shooting ducklings for target practice or specimens (not for food). York's comments to Bynoe led Darwin to suggest that elements of nature, such as ducks, would be avenged for needless killing and that naturally "in a race a little more advanced in culture, the elements would become personified."[93]

In *The Descent of Man...* Darwin repeated the above story, adding that they could never discover that the Fuegians believed "in what we should call a God or practiced any religious rites."[94] Gusinde, on the contrary, was convinced that the Fuegians worshiped a universal god, though in different ways than the Christians. He seemed determined to present evidence that these "stone-age primitives" worshiped Watawineiwa as an "All Mighty." Today Gusinde's hypothesis is subject to doubt. I have the impression that Watawineiwa was supreme in the sense that he (or it) was thought to determine when and where someone would die. Watawineiwa was evoked by chants, imploring a safe passage while canoeing through dangerous waters. And, he or it was scolded and insulted when a child died, as mentioned previously.

Watawineiwa did not create the universe, nor life on earth, nor impose a moral code, as universal gods usually do. The two Yoalox brothers and their sister imposed the moral code and taught people how to hunt and survive.[95] Knowledge of Yamana cosmology is limited, despite Gusinde's contributions, because there is very little information concerning it while the Yamana were still living in their traditional setting (until 1869 when the Anglican missionaries first settled in Yamana territory, on the Isla Grande).

Having found no signs of religious worship, Darwin made this sarcastic remark, recalling Low's testimony of the starving Chonos, "perhaps the muttering of the old man before he distributed the putrid blubber to his famished party, may be of this nature."

Both he and Fitz-Roy affirmed that the Fuegians (the Yamana) had no distinct belief in a future life. According to Gusinde, they believed that the soul or spirit (*keshpi*) of the deceased "outlives the existence of the body." However, one of Gusinde's favorite informants, Nelly Lawrence, clarified that they knew "nothing about the *keshpi* after death."[96]

The Christian paradise, purgatory and hell were certainly not part of their eschatology. The *keshpi* did not live eternally, in the mundane sense of the word, though somehow it existed eternally. It is essential to keep in mind that the most detailed information was obtained very late by Gusinde, in 1920 and 1923, when the surviving Yamanas were somewhat Christianized, working part-time on the sheep farms and struggling to get along in a difficult world, though the elders were still vitally attached to their ancestral culture. The great Chiexaus ceremony was performed for the last time about 1933.

Darwin knew that "Jemmy believed in dreams" because he told Bynoe that he dreamed, on the return voyage of the Beagle in 1832, that his father had died, which turned out to be true (see chapter 4). Darwin was not aware that the shamans had dreams and visions of the "outer world," the mystic universe of the East, from where they derived their power to cure and foresee the future. He evoked the subject of Yamana shamanism in one sentence. "Each family or tribe has a wizard or conjuring doctor, whose office we could never clearly ascertain."

Shamanism is a religion in the measure that it entails beliefs in the existence of supernatural powers that determined or influenced human behavior. Again thanks to Gusinde many of the attributes of the

55

Yamana's particular brand of shamanism become known to the outside world.[97]

Darwin stated that Jemmy "with justifiable pride, stoutly maintained that there was no devil in his land." Darwin found this non-belief remarkable, persuaded as he was that the savage's belief in bad spirits was far more common than in good ones. This simplistic notion is again derived from the cultural evolution paradigm: the "savage," is at the antipodes of the "civilized," though Darwin conceded that the "barbarians" do sometimes independently raise themselves "a few steps in the scale of civilization."[98]

He thought that the Fuegians were not much more superstitious than some of the sailors on the *Beagle* and gave the example of the old quartermaster who affirmed that the heavy gales off Cape Horn were caused by the presence of the Fuegians on board. Here Darwin seems to equate Yahgan beliefs and myths with superstitious notions of the British laboring class. However, the Yahgans were not superstitious, they had a coherent systems of beliefs, a cosmology, which fortunately is partially known.

Perhaps it should be clarified again that Darwin is not being criticized for what he didn't know about the Yamana, for not being an anthropologist. I make additional comments and quote from Gusinde and others to offer the reader a summary view of the Yamana society, in the nineteenth century and the early twentieth when it was studied.

10. NO CHIEFS, NO GOVERNMENT

In his diary for February 6,1833 (while in Wulaia), Darwin explained in more detail what he only mentioned in December 1832 while in Good Success Bay, and briefly in his "meditations."

> The perfect equality of all the inhabitants will for many years prevent their civilization: even a shirt or other article of clothing is immediately torn into pieces. Until some chief rises, who by his power might be able to keep to himself such presents as animals &c &c, there must be an end to all hopes of bettering their condition.

> It would not have been so bad if all the plunder had remained in one family or tribe. But there was a constant succession of fresh canoes, & each one returned with something. Jemmy's own relations were absolutely so foolish & vain, as to show to strangers what they had stolen & the method of doing it.[99]

Here he expressed his conviction that the emergence of civilization could only take place in a society that had a proprietary group of some sort, when socio-economic distinctions were made. In other words, the "perfect equality" and communal sharing of the Yamana prevented them, so to speak, from becoming civilized. But their equality wasn't so perfect, despite their sharing of property and community spirit.

In chapter ten of *The Voyage...* he declared: "The different tribes have no government or chief; yet each is surrounded by other hostile tribes..." In his diary he situated these Fuegians on a zero "scale of governments".

> If the state in which the Fuegians live should be fixed on a zero in the scale of governments, I am afraid the New Zealand [the native Maoris] would rank but a few degrees higher, while Tahiti, even as when first discovered, would occupy a respectable position.

The Yamana did not need chiefs or a government. Their society did not generate a hierarchy of vying political or economic sectors, which in many societies require a tribal chief, a king, a president or a benevolent dictator (if such existed) in order to avoid, mitigate, or control conflicts within the social body. Also, "chiefs" are known to rule for personal interests (benefits) or for those of their family, clan, caste, or class. Though the shamans enjoyed their prestige, they were neither headmen nor chiefs. In this sense, the Yamana society was far more egalitarian than structured societies. They managed without chiefs, police, or jails. The shamans and elders would be heard but they could be disobeyed with no risk of punishment, except during the Chiexaus ceremony (see below). A tolerable order was maintained due to the habit of reciprocity on the model of egalitarian kin networks, the more or less *ad hoc* cooperative groups (for communal hunting and gathering food), and their custom of sharing, that is, due to their community spirit, despite the quarrels. Their myths and the advice of the elders defined right and wrong, and the responsibility of the individual to the family and the community of kin. Their initiation ceremony (the Chiex-aus) taught, inspired, and obliged the youth to apply these principles. If they disobeyed they could be punished by being enforced to comply to a more strict application of the rules, but they were never hurt.[100] No chiefs or government is not a zero point of development, it is attribute of egalitarian societies.

11. "NO FEELING OF HOME"

Darwin: "They cannot know the feeling of having a home, and still less that of domestic affection; for the husband is to the wife a brutal master to a laborious slave."

Here he equated the lack of a home and the lack of domestic affection with the brutality of the husband. They can be treated separately.

First, the Yamana's "haycock" was a temporary shelter, not a home. Hyades pointed out that they also found shelter under a protruding rock or in cave. He emphasized that protecting the fire (and sleeping quarters) was the essential reason for building a hut or locating a shelter. Besides the principal hearth, if the structure or locality was large enough, they might have three or four smaller fires burning so that everyone could find a place near one of them.[101] The wigwam, the other model of a house, was built of logs in the western Alakaluf area, and in Yamana territory, mainly on their islands along Beagle Channel where there were trees with long sturdy trunks. The wigwam was more like a home even though it was also abandoned for months on end when food sources became scarce in the area.

These people were "outdoors" far more than the sedentary British. They were as familiar with a gamut from excellent to less attractive camping sites over many miles through the winding channels, as we are with the rooms of our house or apartment and our neighborhood. Home could be a pebble beach or a pleasant stretch of sand fronted by rocks covered with mussels and lounging seals, some during the winter months, others through the long summer days. Home was also the

13. A Yahgan family in their canoe: painting by Eduardo Armstrong, based on a photograph.

canoe, where the family spent about half its time - the canoe with its fireplace, potable water, a dog or two, domestic and hunting equipment, almost everything essential except a bedroom and a bathroom. Whatever food or material they needed was in the water or along the shore. They often went on land to rest in a "haycock," or to settle for a while, especially during the winter, in a wigwam if possible. They benefited from a stranded whale during weeks or longer when they often performed their ceremonies. They also had to go ashore to manufacture their canoes, for firewood, for material to make their tools, and occasionally to view the landscape from a hilltop. They obtained a few essential items through barter, such as pyrite for igniting a fire. In this sense they were not just "nomads of the sea." They had a strong "feeling of home," an attachment to their territory, both land and sea.

12. "NO DOMESTIC AFFECTION"

Second, the Yamana were a family people; the parents adored, spoiled and respected their children, according to comments of most of the outsiders through the centuries. The husband and wife or wives often didn't remain together "until death do us part" but there were no orphans or outcasts. Everyone had a role and responsibilities in the society, though no one was abandoned or demeaned because he or she was unable to contribute. A generous ingredient of "domestic affection" seems to have prevailed.

13. "THE HUSBAND IS TO THE WIFE A BRUTAL MASTER"

Third, and finally, what was the quality of the man-woman relationship? Darwin observed the Yamana in their canoes, in their camps and on the deck of the *Beagle*. He saw the women paddling their "wretched canoes," patiently fishing in the tangled kelp, gathering shellfish on some forlorn rocky coast, nursing their babies while being dripped on by snow and hail: all this work and hardship, while the men sprang on board the *Beagle*, hands stretched out for whatever was offered. He

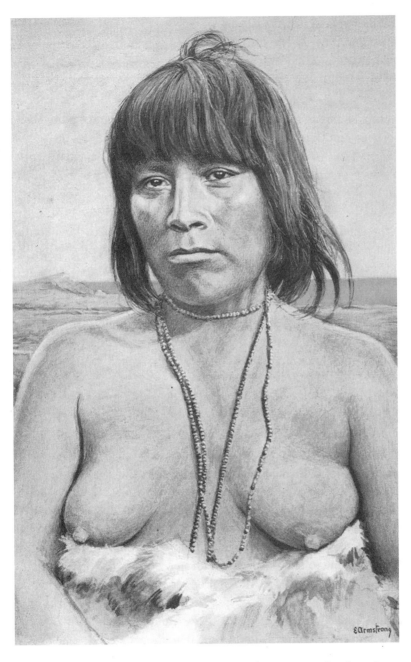

14. A Yamana woman: drawing by Eduardo Armstrong, also based on a photograph.

may also have noticed the males standing in the prow directing the female paddlers, who struggled to decipher their husbands' gestures and shouts. Darwin usually saw the men as opportunists, domineering and exploitative. He didn't see them hunting seals on a rocky coast, grasping cormorants while clinging to a windswept cliff, pealing bark off a tree to construct a canoe, or manufacturing tools. He only saw fleeting moments in the men's lives, though he did notice them hard at work for Fitz-Roy in Wulaia (see below).

Both sexes contributed to the essential labor (the shamans worked like everyone else). But whether or not the labor was equally portion out is another matter. Martin Gusinde thought it was. Note that the women performed the most time consuming, daily tasks. Besides care of the children and paddling the canoe, they spent a great deal of time fishing from their canoes, and collecting shellfish, berries, birds' eggs, mushrooms, and fungi, though the children usually helped. They wove sturdy baskets and softened animal skins. They as well as the men collected firewood that often didn't need cutting because of the abundance of rotting and dead timber in the forests. Adolescents of both sexes underwent the prolonged initiation ceremony, the Chiexaus, though the young men were obliged, or privileged, to partake in an additional one, called the Kina.

Darwin and others, compared the men to slave masters mainly because they were often seen taking it easy while the women were hard at work. They had more leisure than the women during nineteenth century than before because the British and Yankee fishermen had diminished the seal and whale population. Recall that by the time of Darwin (1833-34) the Yamana relied more on fish, mussels and other shellfish (which were mainly procured by the women) than on seals and whales. Though some seals had survived and whales were occasionally beached, they were far less abundant than they had been, thus the men had more time to take it easy than formerly.

Note that the men's work required more training than the women's labor and this probably always gave them certain superiority. When speed was required they paddled the canoe and could gather food though perhaps with less know-how than the women. The men fished with a net while the women only used bate without a hook. The women did not know how make tools, hunt cormorants or seals or manufacture a canoe. The men had probably always had more leisure and, with few exceptions, held the positions of prestige as shamans (*yekamush* - spiritual leaders and healers), and as directors of the ceremonies. Nor did husbands always treat their wives kindly. If a wife was abused she could seek help with her original family or kin group but this might prove too difficult for her to achieve. Some husbands, such as Jemmy, were very attached to their spouses and children, though gender inequality existed during Darwin's visits and probably before. However, the men were not "brutal masters" of the women as Darwin contended.

14. "THEIR SKILL [WAS LIKE]... THE INSTINCT OF ANIMALS"

Darwin punctuated his belittling thoughts about the Fuegians with a reference to John Byron (the poet's grandfather). In his 1741 report of an experience as a castaway in the Gulf of Peñas area (Alakaluf territory) he saw "a wretched mother pick up her bleeding dying infant-boy, whom her husband had mercilessly dashed on the stones for dropping a basket of sea-eggs!." This horror story may be true. It made Darwin wonder: "How little can the higher powers of the mind be brought into play...to knock a limpet from the rock does not require even cunning, that lowest power of the mind." These remarks in turn reminded Darwin of the Yahgan canoe: "Their skill in some respects may be compared to the instinct of animals...the canoe, their most ingenious work, poor as it is, has remained the same, as we know from Drake, for the last two hundred and fifty years."[102]

The Yahgan did not contribute to the sophistication of the great civilizations, or the inventiveness of the Renaissance, or the incipient Industrial Revolution. Modern science was still in their future, if future they were to have. Darwin was aware of this but even so he didn't attempt to understand their mode of living, much less admire their mastery of a difficult environment, nor was he aware that their best-made canoes were "non-perfectible" (my term), the very best that could be fashioned given the materials available and their isolation "at the end of the earth." Brian Street, a literary historian, made this point: "Primitive peoples are considered to be slaves of custom and thus to be unable to break with the despotism of their own 'collective conscience'."[103]

15. BUT WHY DID THESE FUEGIANS
SETTLE AT THIS END OF NO-WHERE?

Darwin wondered:

> Whilst beholding these savages, one asks, whence have
> they come? What could have tempted, or what change
> compelled a tribe of men, to leave the fine regions of the
> north, to travel down the Cordillera or backbone of Amer-
> ica, to invent and build canoes, which are not used by the
> tribes of Chile, Peru and Brazil, and then to enter on one
> of the most inhospitable countries within the limits of the
> globe?[104]

This question is still being asked today. Look up the works of the
archeologists Julius Bird, José Luis Orquera, Ernesto Piana, and
Dominique Legoupil. They have found valid answers, which again con-
tradict Darwin.

Despite this "inhospitable country":

> There is no reason to believe that the Fuegians decrease in
> number: therefore we must suppose that they enjoy a suf-
> ficient share of happiness, of whatever kind it may be, to
> render life worth having.

This amazing comment is by Darwin, who expressed little empathy
for these "savages." But in the next sentence he took the romance out
of this thought: "Nature by making habit omnipotent, and its effects
hereditary, has fitted the Fuegian to the climate and the productions of
his miserable country."[105]

16. DARWIN'S LEGACY: A MISERABLE PEOPLE FIT
A MISERABLE COUNTRY

It overshadowed his recognition that after all they were mentally on
a par with the rest of humanity. Years later in *The Descent of Man...* he
affirmed:

The Fuegians rank among the lowest barbarians; but I was continually struck with surprise how closely the three natives on board H.M.S. 'Beagle,' who had lived some years in England, and could talk a little English, resembled us in disposition and in most of our mental faculties.

And again:

I was incessantly struck while living with the Fuegians on board the 'Beagle' with the many little traits of character showing how similar their minds were to ours; and so it was with the full-blooded Negro with whom I happened once to be intimate.[106]

Even though he considered the three Fuegians (Fuegia, Jemmy and York) his equals, he never altered his original impression of their people as "the lowest barbarians." Rather than explain that, after all, Darwin's attitude towards them was an expression of the prevailing "mind set" of his epoch, it is revealing to recall that his British contemporaries such as the sealers Weddell and Webster (the medical doctor in Foster's expedition) were more open-minded than he was and more inclined to recognize the Yamana as fellow human beings. Though Webster was an intellectual neither he nor Weddell were aware that these Fuegians could be classified as the lowest on the scale of humanity.

Ernst Mayr, one of the most outstanding biologists of the "New Synthesis," made a somewhat similar comment with reference to the immediate success of *On the Origin of Species*. "Curiously at that time the concept appealed particularly to laymen. Those who were best informed about biology, and especially about classification and morphology, upheld most strongly the dogma of creation and the constancy of species." Those who were "best informed" opposed Darwin. Mayr insisted: "It is Darwin, and Darwin alone, who deserves the credit for having changed this situation overnight."[107]

This ends the review of Darwin's "ethnological meditations" and the comments they have inspired.

CHAPTER 4

DARWIN MEETS THE YAHGANS AT HOME: 1833

1. THE WORST STORM THEY EVER ENCOUNTERED: JANUARY 1 - 13

Darwin and the others were "tired and impatient by the delay caused by bad weather," when the *Beagle* finally departed from the Saint Martin's Cove, the last day of 1832. Fitz-Roy intended to land York and Fuegia among their own people (the Alakaluf), on Waterman Island (near York Minster cliff, along Christmas Sound), as he had promised them. Heading in that direction, the *Beagle* was keeping close to the islands when suddenly she was thrown out to sea, swept into a relentless succession of gales, strong winds and high seas.

Three days later she had drifted in the opposite direction, southwest to 57° 23' lat. S (Cape Horn is at 55° 59' lat. S), Fitz-Roy remained undaunted. "Our good little ship weathered them cleverly, going from seven and a half to eight knots an hour, under close-reefed topsails and double-reefed courses, the top-gallant-masts being on deck."[108]

But the *Beagle* was still "heavily pitching" seven days later. Darwin was anxious. "I have scarcely for an hour been quite free from sea-sickness... my spirits, temper & stomach, I am well assured, will not hold out much longer."

On January 11 a more violent squall struck near the wild-looking York Minster cliff. The surf was "breaking fearfully on the coast," spray

67

was seen rising over the cliff about 200 feet high, as the crew struggled to shorten the sails. The rampaging squall didn't let up. Darwin noted: "On the 12th the gale was very heavy, and we did not know exactly where we were, it was a most unpleasant sound to hear constantly repeated. 'Keep a good look-out to leeward'." Prone to sea-sickness even in calm weather, he was yearning for the "warm serene air & the beautiful forms of the Tropics."[109]

The storm kept raging all the next morning "with its full fury," as the ship lurched deeply. At noon the sea "broke over us...the poor Beagle trembled at the shock, but soon, like a good ship that she was, she righted and came up to the wind again." Soon after 1 p.m. the sea rose to even greater heights. Fitz-Roy became really alarmed. "I was anxiously watching the successive waves, when three huge rollers approached, whose size and steepness at once told me that our sea-boat, good as she was, would be sorely tried." The third huge roller plunged the *Beagle* two or three feet under water, from the cathead to the stern, and one of the "beautiful whale-boats" had to be cut away. This was the worst gale Fitz-Roy had ever experienced. Darwin thought this moment might be his last. "Had another sea followed the first, our fate would have been decided soon, and for ever." The sea struck yet again but the crisis was passing.[110]

The sea calmed down, about 4 p.m. that day, but the *Beagle* was off her course. Fitz-Roy steered her to the nearest known land position, False Cape Horn, at the southern extremity of Hoste Island. The next day Darwin lamented:

> I have suffered an irreparable loss from yesterday's disaster, in my drying paper & plants being wetted with salt-water. Nothing resists the force of a heavy sea; it forces open doors & sky lights, & spread universal damage. None but those who have tried it, know the miseries of a really heavy gale of wind. May Providence keep the Beagle out of them.

As they pulled in along the False Cape, Darwin exclaimed: "How delightful was that still night, after having been so long involved in the din of the warring elements!"[111]

Darwin's collections, in the poop and forecastle cabins on deck, were "much injured." The *Beagle* had nearly gone under on that 13th of January 1833. Five months later Darwin recalled these moments in a letter to his cousin William Darwin Fox.

> We had plenty of very severe gales of wind: one beating match of 3 weeks off the Horn; when it often blew so hard, you could scarcely look at it. We shipped a sea - which spoiled all my paper for drying plants: oh the miseries of a real gale of wind![112]

Fitz-Roy informed Captain Beaufort, in the London office, that this storm convinced him that Anson (in 1741) had not exaggerated when he described the fury of the sea while rounding Cape Horn and that a disaster had been avoided, thanks to the good condition of the *Beagle*. "None of my Shipmates saw so much furious wind during the previous five years in the Beagle. Five vessels have been wrecked on 'Terra Del' [Fuego] and at the Falklands."[113]

2. VIA BEAGLE CHANNEL IN A CARAVAN, DARWIN IS PLEASED: JANUARY 19 – 22

Fitz-Roy had decided to take Jemmy home first and leave off Fuegia and York in Waterman Island later, so he rounded False Cape Horn and sailed up Nassau Bay in search of a harbor near Beagle Channel. On January 15 he anchored the *Beagle* in Goree Road, off the southeastern corner of Navarin Island, the haven discovered by the Dutch in 1624. He praised it as "one of the most spacious, accessible and safe anchorages in these regions." Everyone rested, during the next four days, from those two weeks of rugged sea and took turns preparing the ship for her next destination.

Then York informed him that he and Fuegia had decided to stay with Jemmy, in his home territory, in Woollya (now spelt Wulaia), on the west coast of Navarin Island. Fitz-Roy was relieved. Except for the death of Boat Memory, he was keeping his promise of returning the Fuegians to their homeland, in good health and with plenty of gifts. If York and Fuegia preferred to be let off in Jemmy's territory, instead of being taken to their own territory, all the better. The three appeared content to have put their trust in him.

For this happy occasion, Fitz-Roy decided to escort them to Jemmy's territory twenty-nine members of the crew. Besides Darwin and the future missionary Matthews, he chose Bynoe, lieutenants Hamond, Stewart, Johnson, and twenty-four seamen. James Bennett, Jemmy's good friend, was one of the party, though Fitz-Roy didn't mention him. All were to be taken in three whaleboats and a yawl (a sailing boat, equipped with two masts), a veritable caravan. A deck had to be installed on the yawl for the heavy cargo of gifts. She could be pulled along by the whaleboats, if the wind turned adverse. The *Beagle* with the rest of the crew was to await their return in Goree Road.[114]

The caravan set out from Goree Road up the east coast of Navarin, on January 19 (1833). It was not long before the over-loaded yawl had to be towed by the three whaleboats being rowed against the wind and current. When they rounded the northeastern corner of Navarin Island, Beagle Channel came into full view. Fitz-Roy was impressed:

> To the westward we saw an immense canal, looking like a work of gigantic art, extending between parallel ranges of mountains, of which the summits were capped with snow, though their sides were covered by endless forests. This singular canal-like passage is almost straight and of near-ly uniform width (overlooking minute details) for one hun-dred and twenty miles.[115]

Darwin was more laconic: "This channel...is a most remarkable fea-ture in the geography of this, or indeed of any other country." He com-pared it to Lochness, a valley in Scotland, which he had probably vis-ited.[116]

Fitz-Roy hadn't sailed in Beagle Channel, since May 1830, though sealers and whalers had certainly penetrated it before. The party went ashore in a "snug little cove," pitched their tents and relaxed, that evening, January 19. Darwin was delighted.

> Nothing could look more comfortable than this scene. The glassy water of the little harbour, with the branches of the trees hanging over the rocky beach, the boats at anchors,

the tents supported by the crossed oars, and the smoke curling up the wooded valley, formed a picture of quiet retirement.[117]

As they sailed and rowed west along Beagle Channel, through MacKinlay Pass where the channel narrows down from some three miles to about one because a rather large island, later named Gable, obstructs it.

3. DARWIN MEETS THE YAHGANS (YAMANAS) AT HOME

Recall that I use the terms Yahgan and Yamana interchangeably. Although Yahgan is the local name for those in Jemmy's territory and the vicinity, both terms apply to the entire group.

Darwin observed: "We began to enter today the parts of the country which are thickly inhabited." Along the coast "the constant succession of fresh objects quite takes away the fatigue of sitting so many hours in one position."[118] The fires, which the Yahgans had lit to greet the "little fleet," reminded Darwin of the meaning of Tierra del Fuego, so named because in 1520, when the Strait of Magellan was discovered, the natives there made fires along the coasts to spread the news of the arrival of Magellan's huge "canoe." Now these natives, (the Yahgans) looked so astonished that Darwin thought that most of them had never seen white men before. They ran for miles along the shore, hailing the strangers. Darwin was amazed.

> I shall never forget how wild and savage one group appeared: suddenly four or five men came to the edge of an overhanging cliff [of Gable Island]; they were absolutely naked, and their long hair streamed about their faces; they held rugged staffs in their hands, and, springing from the ground, they waved their arms around their heads, and sent forth the most hideous yells.

Their appearance was "so strange, that is was scarcely like that of earthly inhabitants."

Further down the channel, which broadens out again beyond MacKinlay Pass, on the south shore (Navarin Island), the natives were clutching their slings and seemed "not inclined to be friendly." But once the crew landed, they became delighted by the "trifling presents," especially the biscuits and the red cloths that they immediately tied around their heads. While Darwin was having lunch,

> one of the savages touched with his finger some of the meat preserved in tin cases which I was eating, and feeling it soft and cold, showed as much disgust at it, as I should have done at putrid blubber.

Everyone probably laughed at the expression of disgust on the "savage's" face, except Jemmy who "was thoroughly ashamed."[119]

Here Jemmy was among people of his own culture and language for the first time since he had departed two and a half years earlier. However, he clarified that these were not his friends, not his "tribe," and that they often made war on his people. York laughed at them, shouting "large monkeys," and, to add insult to injury, "yapoos" (otters). Fuegia hid and refused to look at them a second time. Jemmy insisted that they were "not at all like my people, who are very good and clean." Fitz-Roy had a different opinion. "Jemmy's own tribe was as inferior in every way as the worst of those whom he and York called 'monkeys - dirty - fools - not men'." Darwin became visibly annoyed at their insistent demands for presents, even the buttons on his coat, and their annoying shouts of *yammerschooner* that he thought meant "give me." According to the missionary Thomas Bridges, this expression signified "be kind to us."[120] In this situation *yammerschooner*, may have meant "give me," as well as "be kind to us."

4. JEMMY'S BAD NEIGHBORS: DARWIN "MUCH AFRAID..."

The morning of January 21, other canoes had landed nearby, where the crew was camping on Navarin Island (the south coast of Beagle Channel). The men jumped out of their canoes and started picking up stones on the shore while their women and children rushed into the forest. Darwin was "much afraid" not for himself or his shipmates but because had a skirmish resulted "it would have been shocking to have fired on such naked miserable creatures."

> Like wild beasts, they do not appear to compare numbers; for each individual, if attacked, instead of retiring, will endeavour to dash your brains out with a stone, as certainly as a tiger under similar circumstances would tear you.

Fitz-Roy also became anxious as the tension mounted. They laughed at him as he flourished a cutlass (a short slightly curved sword). He fired his pistol twice close to one native who looked astounded and rubbed his head. Darwin surmised afterwards that someone who is ignorant of firearms might not realize their killing power. Even when he sees the wound caused by a bullet "it may be some time before he is able at all to understand how it is effected; for the fact of a body [the bullet] being invisible from its velocity would perhaps be to him an idea totally inconceivable." Jemmy refused to go ashore to greet these bad neighbors.

By morning Fitz-Roy became really aggravated by the unfriendly gestures of this "hostile tribe," and ordered his men to return to the ship and cross her over to the north side of the channel (Isla Grande). Darwin agreed. "They are such thieves & so bold Cannibals that one naturally prefers separate quarters." But the hostile natives pursued them, paddling their canoes at full speed, which aggravated Fitz-Roy all the more. The caravan kept ahead, struggling against a strong breeze and tide. Finally free of the pursuers, the crew landed the caravan on the north shore near a forest that had been burning over many leagues, so many that it had been mistaken for a volcanic eruption by a ship passing Cape Horn.[121]

The next day, January 22, they were favored by beautiful weather. Darwin was impressed:

> The mountains were here [Isla Grande] about three thousand feet high, and terminated in sharp and jagged points. They rose in one unbroken sweep from the water's edge, and were covered to the height of fourteen or fifteen hundred feet by the dusky-coloured forest.

Here he undoubtedly referred to the mountains behind the bay of Ushuaia, the location of a large Yamana camping site, where the missionaries first settled in 1869 and the Argentine navy founded in 1884, the present city of the same name.

5. NO-MAN'S LAND

No natives were seen then or when they passed back to the opposite shore, to Navarin Island. Jemmy explained to Fitz-Roy that this was the "land between bad people and his friends." Darwin also reported, that it appeared to be neutral (uninhabited) ground.

> After an unmolested night in what would appear to be neutral ground, between Jemmy's tribe and the people we saw yesterday, we sailed pleasantly along. I do not know anything which shows more clearly the hostile state of the different tribes, than these wide borders or neutral tracts. Although Jemmy Button well knew the force of our party, he was, at first, unwilling to land amidst the hostile tribe nearest to his own.[122]

The unoccupied territory lay between the hostile Yamanas and Jemmy's friends, further west. The "hostile natives" lived on both shores of the Beagle Channel, in the area of the present city Ushuaia on the north shore. However, those living further east, beyond Beagle Channel, on Picton, Lennox and New islands were friendly. Jemmy did not call them "bad people."

6. JEMMY'S FRIENDS

They anchored the boats that evening further along the shore of Navarin Island, near the entrance to Murray Narrows, named for Master Murray who discovered it during the first Beagle voyage in April 1830. They were probably in Lewaia (also spelt Lauwaia) Cove near the present town of Puerto Navarino. Here it was only a few hours pull to one of Jemmy's camp sites, Wulaia, located south of the narrows, along Ponsonby Sound.[123]

Three men and two women fled when the crew went ashore. Two sailors approached the men quietly and reassured them, so they returned, seemingly at ease, to greet the strangers. Jemmy was now among friends, near where he had been abducted nearly two years and six months earlier, during the first voyage, mid-May 1830. Fitz-Roy thought the friends' manner of speaking softer and less guttural than that of the "bad men," found them much better disposed, though "as abject and degraded in outward appearance as any Fuegians I had ever seen." He was surprised, and perhaps amused, that Jemmy seemed to have almost forgotten his native tongue whereas York appeared to understand what the friends were saying, though he didn't speak their language.[124]

Jemmy had not forgotten his native language. He understood immediately when the friendly men told him that his mother and siblings were well but that his father had died during his absence. Fitz-Roy commented: "Poor Jemmy looked very grave and mysterious at the news, but showed no other symptom of sorrow." He had told his friends Bynoe and Bennett, on the return voyage, that a man had come to the side of his hammock and whispered to him that his father had died. He had first mentioned this dream to Bynoe, who tried to laugh him out of the idea. Fitz-Roy commented: "He fully believed that such was the case, and maintained his opinion up to the time of finding that his father had died."

After hearing the confirmation of the sad news, Jemmy gathered some branches, made a fire and solemnly watched them burn. Following this rather brief meditation he was talking and laughing as usual. He never mentioned his father's death again.[125] Neither Fitz-Roy nor Darwin knew that, as a sign of respect, the Yamana should not evoke or speak about the deceased in public.

7. YORK, THE JEALOUS SUITOR

The weather was "so warm" (53° F) that several of the crew bathed in Beagle Channel. That evening, the seamen kidded York so incessantly about his "intended wife," that he became angry with one of his best friends who was among the teasers. Fitz-Roy had noticed that York was excessively jealous of Fuegia.

If any one spoke to her, he watched every word; if he was
not sitting by her side, he grumbled sulkily; but if he was
accidentally separated, and obliged to go in a different
boat, his behaviour became sullen and morose.[126]

Darwin remarked that the three local men were "quiet and inoffensive." They gathered near the blazing fire as evening set in, while the two women retired to their wigwam, near the tents the crew had set up. The seamen, though well clothed and sitting beside the fire, were "far from too warm; yet these naked savages, though further off, were...steaming with perspiration at undergoing such a roasting." Despite the roasting, they joined in the singing but invariably a little behind, which Darwin found "quite ludicrous."

8. JEMMY'S FEAR OF THE OENS-MEN

Everyone was gathered around the campfire, during the evenings of the 21st and 22nd, while Jemmy told long stories about the Oens-men. Darwin noted:

He often told us how the savage Oens-men 'when the leaf
red' [autumn, September to December], they crossed the
mountains from the eastern coast of Tierra del Fuego, and
made inroads on the natives of this part of the country.
It was most curious to watch him when thus talking, and
see his eyes gleaming and his whole face assume a new
and wild expression.[127]

Darwin clarified that the Oens-men were "tall men, the foot Patagonians of the East coast." Recall that the Oens-men (Onas) were the Selk'nam, the "foot people," guanaco hunters and warriors.

Jemmy said that almost every year these Oens-men "make desperate inroads upon the Tekeenica [Yahgan] 'tribe,' carrying off women and children, dogs, arrows, spears, and canoes; and killing the men whom they succeed in making prisoners." He insisted that these Oens-men made annual excursions at the time of the "red leaf." Fitz-Roy explained that during the autumn the mountains (the border between the Selk'-

nam and the Yamana on Isla Grande) were least difficult to pass. These Oens-men would sometimes came, "in parties from fifty to a hundred," over the mountains down to the shore of Beagle Channel where they seized canoes belonging to the Yapoos (here Jemmy referred to the Yahgans who were not allies of the Oens-men). Then they paddling these canoes across Beagle Channel, having fastened (tied) them together to avoid being separated. Once they landed, on Navarin Island, they drove "the smaller and much inferior Tekeenica people before them in every direction. By Jemmy's account there are hard battles sometimes and the Oens tribe lose men…" Fitz-Roy added that they seemed to be the strongest because they always managed to carry away their dead. He explained: "These periodical invasions of…[the Oens-men]…are not to be confounded with the frequent disputes and skirmished which take place between the Tekeenica tribes [the "bad people" of Jemmy's group]." Jemmy's stories were so often repeated in different contexts that they ring true.[128]

9. AN ADVANCE PARTY ARRIVES "LIKE SO MANY DEMONIACS…"

Just as the caravan was about to embark for Wulaia, the next morning (January 23), Fitz-Roy was startled when he noticed several natives running towards the caravan from the nearby hills. They were "breathless with haste, perspiring violently, and bleeding at the nose. Startled by their appearance, we thought they had been fighting." The image of devils came again to Darwin's mind.

> Several of them had run so fast that their noses were bleeding, and their mouths frothed from the rapidity with which they talked; and with their naked bodies all bedaubed with black, white and red, they looked like so many demoniacs who had been fighting.

They soon learned that the men were bleeding because of the exertion of running and that they had come from Wulaia to greet Jemmy. (Word of the caravan in the channel had gotten around fast.) Fitz-Roy remained vigilant despite their friendly disposition while Jemmy calmly told them about his trip and explained the motives of the visiting strangers. All of them belonged to Jemmy's district, except one who Jemmy said was an "Oens-man," a hostage in Wulaia though Fitz-Roy believed he belonged to the "hostile" Tekeenica (Yahgan) tribe.

10. DOWN MURRAY NARROWS, "A SCENE WHICH CARRIED ONE'S THOUGHTS TO THE SOUTH SEA ISLANDS"

Twelve canoes suddenly appeared paddling towards them from every direction and the caravan's departure was detained again. Darwin counted four to five men in each canoe. Their deep voices rang out from the distance welcoming the caravan. In the midst of all the joyous shouting, the runners from Wulaia echoed their greetings. Fitz-Roy urged his men to speed up the preparations lest the ever-increasing traffic obstruct their departure. When he noticed the twelve canoes escorting his caravan as it pulled off the shore down Murray Narrows, he was not worried about all the commotion because all the men were Jemmy's friends. The beauty of the surroundings impressed him: first the deep blue water of Beagle Channel flanked by the snow-covered mountains of Hoste Island then the "cheerful sunny woodland, sloping gradually down to the Murray Narrows."

Thirty or forty more canoes appeared paddling eagerly towards the caravan as it glided through the narrows, the men greeting the caravan again with "the full power of [their] deep sonorous voices. Columns of blue smoke rose from the small fires in the canoes while their voices resounded off the nearby cliffs, creating echoes of continual cheer." What a truly magnificent cortege accompanied Darwin for his first visit to Jemmy's homeland. (Fitz-Roy had passed through the narrows twice in 1830 with no fanfare.)

Having passed through the narrows, the caravan reached the wooded islets (namely the large island, later called Button Island, in Ponsonby Sound), where even more canoes joined them. The sailors were pulling hard in the four boats. advancing well ahead of their enthusiastic cortege when Fitz-Roy mused: "The day being very fine, without a breeze to ruffle the water, it was a scene which carried one's thoughts to the South Sea Islands but in Tierra del Fuego almost appeared like a dream."[129]

15. Wulaia. Three Fuegians (Yahgans) and their dog seated on the shore of Wulaia: drawing by Conrad Martens.

11. THE FIRST DAY IN WULAIA;
EVERYONE IS PLEASED: JANUARY 23

Darwin remarked: "Jemmy was now in a district well known to him, and guided the boats to a quiet pretty cove named Woollya [Wulaia], surrounded by islets, every one of which and every point had its proper native name."[130]

Fitz-Roy and his men "were much pleased by the situation of Woollya, and Jemmy was very proud of the praises bestowed upon his land." Indeed Wulaia merited praises for its pastures of thick grass and wild flowers, its brooks meandering down to the coast backed by rolling hills where guanacos used to roam. Small wooded offshore islands enhance the view across Ponsonby Sound, where the distant snow capped mountains of Hoste Island emerge. This is an image of Wulaia as I saw it in February 1987, except for unsightly cement buildings, that had been constructed as a radio station by the Chilean navy, probably in the 1930s. It was not inhabited in 1987, nor were any guanacos grazing on the hillsides.

12. FITZ-ROY MARKS OFF A NO-TRESPASSING ZONE

A few native men came to greet the caravan, while the women and children scattered. Darwin clarified that they were "a family of Jemmy's tribe, but not his relations." Fitz-Roy selected a clear space to install the tents, facing the shore. The boats were moored nearby in case they might be urgently needed. He ordered his men to trace a line on the ground with spades, between the tents and the grassland beyond, as an added precaution. Meanwhile, more local natives had arrived and were informed (by gestures) not to pass over the line. Then he placed some of his men as sentries, seated or standing along the line and ordered them to guard it. He was very concerned about his numerical inferiority. Having designated the no-trespassing zone, he prepared to receive his hosts, the local men, who were (or had become) reticent. Soon the natives in the canoes that had followed the caravan "began to pour in." The men joined the crowd while their women and children sat at a distance near their canoes. More canoes kept arriving and soon there were

16. My photograph, taken in 1987, of the small islands off shore of Wulaia.

over a hundred visitors. These men immediately sent their women and children to the abandoned wigwams further inland while they thronged along the boundary line where they were signaled to halt. Finally, thanks to the good temper of the crew who continued handing out presents and, Fitz-Roy added, to "the broken Fuegian explanations of our dark-coloured shipmates [York and Jemmy], we succeeded in getting the natives squatted on their hams around the line."[131]

A "no trespassing line," in their own land guarded by strangers, must have puzzled some of them and perhaps outraged others (see below). This was their first hint of the invasions to come, but they had no way of foreseeing such a future.

13. THE WORK BEGINS

While Fitz-Roy was inspecting the set-up, Jemmy was becoming increasingly out of sorts by the quizzing of his countrymen, though he continued distributing nails and tools to them. But soon he was kept busy with York and the sailors, chopping wood, clearing the ground for one of the two gardens (that would be planted) and constructing three wigwams: the largest for Matthews, another for Jemmy and the third for York and Fuegia, who were already considered a couple, though Fuegia was only about twelve years old. Darwin observed that a the "women took much notice of and were very kind to Fuegia."[132]

Fitz-Roy and his men were aware that they were even more outnumbered than when they landed, but by sunset all the visiting natives departed in their canoes. He wondered if they were planning some mischief. He soon realized that they were probably not planning to attack, given the friendly manner they had accepted the "no trespassing line," which he attributed to York's and Fuegia's visits to the wigwams.

A bit later that evening, a canoe was sent to "Button Island," where Jemmy's family was said to be residing. (This name was first used at this time and since appears on all the maps.)

14. THE SECOND DAY, JEMMY IS REUNITED WITH HIS FAMILY

Early the next morning, January 24, a deep voice was heard repeatedly coming from a small canoe, over a mile away. [133] Jemmy exclaimed "my brother!" shouting to Fitz-Roy that it was the voice of his oldest brother, as he climbed a rock on the shore watching the canoe slowly approaching. Darwin remarked on the great distance from which Jemmy identified the voice, adding: "To be sure their voices are wonderfully powerful...All the organs of sense are highly perfected." Then he recalled: "When Jemmy quarreled with any of the officers [on the *Beagle* during the return trip], he would say 'me see ship, me no tell.' Both he & York have invariably been in the right, even when objects have been examined with a glass [binoculars]." [134]

Jemmy advanced slowly to greet his mother, two sisters, and three brothers as the canoe pushed onto the shore. He didn't learn any details about his father's death "as his relations would not speak about it." His mother only glanced at him as she hastened to secure the canoe and hide a basket she was carrying. Later Fitz-Roy discovered that her basket contained "all she possessed: tinder, fire-stone, paint, etc, and a bundle of fish." Jemmy's two sisters ran to catch up with their mother without looking back at him while his brothers (an adult and two grown boys) stared at him for a moment and then walked around him in complete silence. Fitz-Roy was amazed. "Animals when they meet show far more animation and anxiety than were displayed at this meeting." Darwin was more emphatic. "The meeting was less interesting than that between a horse, turned out into a field, when he joins an old companion." [135] Because there was no demonstration of affection, they surmised there was none, but for the Yamana such behavior was custom; one should not show emotions on these occasions.

When Jemmy's elder brother talked to him, he did not reply at first, though he did finally - in English. Darwin deduced "that Jemmy had almost forgotten his own language," and commented that "his English was very imperfect. It was laughable, but almost pitiable, to hear him speak to his wild brother in English, and then ask him in Spanish (*'no sabe?'*) whether he did not understand him." [136] Jemmy had probably picked up some Spanish from sealers before Fitz-Roy abducted him (in May 1830) and was now showing off his English to his brother.

15. JEMMY, TOMMY, HARRY AND BILLY BUTTON

None of the "Button boys" would fit the missionaries' model of the ideal native. Jemmy remained loyal through the years to Fitz-Roy, his British friends, and Darwin. His relations with the missionaries were also personal, not religious. Tommy, despite his loving personality, disappointed them. Harry remained in the background, while the youngest, Billy, reappeared during the massacre of 1859, as related above. Jemmy's sisters also reappeared: the youngest was mistaken for his third wife and lived with his family while and his older sister became the mother of a great favorite of the head missionary, Thomas Bridges. No portraits of them were found and only two sketches of Jemmy (by Fitz-Roy).

16. YORK TELLS DARWIN SOME STARTLING NEWS

York's comments to Darwin may surprise the reader though Darwin did not grasp their significance.

> We heard, however, that the mother had been inconsolable for the loss of Jemmy, and had searched everywhere for him, thinking that he might have been left [somewhere on the island] after having been taken in the boat.[137]

York was referring to May 13, 1830, the day Jemmy climbed on Fitz-Roy's cutter, near Lewaia, and the entrance to Murray Narrows. York's comments prove that Jemmy was taken (to England) without his mother's knowledge or consent and presumably without his father's, in other words, Fitz-Roy had kidnapped him, though not forcefully. That day of May 1830, when Jemmy was on board Fitz-Roy's cutter pulling into the narrows, he may have thought that in a short while he would be let off somewhere nearby. Or perhaps, being a child of thirteen or so, he may have thought it was fun, a new adventure. That same day, when he boarded the *Beagle* (in Lennox Cove), York, Fuegia and Boat Memory probably reassured him that he was in good company, even though they greeted him by calling him a *yapoo*, an otter. Somehow he and the other three understood, by signs, that they were to be carried off, far from their homeland.

17. THE THIRD DAY IN WULAIA, GOOD NEIGHBORS RETURN: JANUARY 25

Some of the neighbors returned in their canoes the next day and rapidly pitched in helping the crew build the three wigwams and plant cabbage, potatoes, peas and turnips. Such vegetables were unknown to the Yahgans who, moreover, were much fonder of fish and meat than any root or plant, except certain mushrooms that they did relish. Fitz-Roy probably imagined that they would learn to like the vegetables and that the gardens would encourage them to adopt a more sedentary (and civilized) routine of living. Meanwhile other canoes arrived for the first time. The newcomers also joined in the labor, bringing wood and bundles of grass to thatch the wigwams. With all this help, the three wigwams were nearly finished. York was very pleased with his wigwam, with Wulaia and with all the activity. He assured Fitz-Roy that Jemmy's eldest brother, Tom, was "very much friend," the country a "very good land" and repeated his wish to settle there.

Jemmy had given his brothers nails, tools and English clothes and the latter to his sisters and mother. Fitz-Roy presented his mother with a garment. She reciprocated with a large quantity of fish. Later Jemmy escorted her to visit Fitz-Roy, dressed in her new outfit. He was informed that Jemmy's eldest brother, Tom or Tommy, was a "doctor" (in reality a *yekamush*, a shaman) who, despite his young age (early twenties) "was held in high estimation among his own tribe." Fitz-Roy explained that his occupation involved pretending to identify and to cure illnesses.[138] On this third day, several seamen and probably Darwin went hunting in the nearby hills but the guanacos, the only prey, were so wild that they could not be killed even with firearms. Also, Fitz-Roy met an important person, the older Dr Button, Jemmy's uncle (his father's brother), and some "strangers" arrived.

18. TOO MANY "STRANGERS": JANUARY 26

Then more visitors arrived, "bad people - no friends," according to Jemmy. Fitz-Roy called them the "Yapoo Tekeenica tribe", meaning they were "bad-otter" Yahgans. Jemmy had adopted the derogatory *yapoo* (otter) term for his Beagle Channel neighbors, his Yahgan enemies, while York used it for all the Yahgans. But Tekeenica is not a word at all; it is a phrase in the Yahgan language that Fitz-Roy mistook for the name of the natives, during his first voyage.[139]

Darwin calculated that "at one time" there were 120 strangers (including the peaceful neighbors) present in Wulaia while Fitz-Roy wrote that on January 26 more than 300 were there.[140] This discrepancy may be explained by the fact that not all of them arrived together and therefore their numbers were estimated at different times. Also these numbers were guesses as there is no indication that the "heads" were counted.

Fitz-Roy wrote that the many who had arrived were "strangers to Jemmy's family," that his brothers and mother had no influence over them and that they "cared for them as little as they did for us, and were intent only upon plunder."[141] These strangers were not Oens-men, for if they had been Jemmy would have been more alarmed. They were his enemy neighbors.

19. THE BATHING SCENE

Neither Fitz-Roy nor Darwin witnessed this scene, though both recorded it. Quite a few of the seamen were bathing in a nearby stream while several natives sat by peacefully looking on, much amused by their white skin and "the act of washing." While this admiring was going on, some of the admirers absconded with the bathers' handkerchiefs, shoes and whatever else looked interesting. Darwin noted: "They asked for every thing they saw & stole what they could." Fitz-Roy arrived late and put an end to these "ablutions" without offending anyone.[142]

That evening York and Fuegia retired to their new home. Jemmy to his new wigwam and Matthews slept in one of the boats. By then the crew had almost finished the solid floor of boards, under which Matthews intended to safeguard his most valuable belongings.

20. PRACTICE SHOOTING BEFORE DARK

That same evening (daylight lasted until past midnight), the crew practiced firing at a target with three objectives: keeping the weapons in condition, "exercising the men – and aweing [sic], without frightening the natives." Fitz-Roy was still worried about his numerical inferiority: the 300, compared to his twenty-nine. He calculated that that two-thirds of them had never seen a gun. The public, mostly the strangers, sat watching "eagerly talking to each other, as successful shots were made at the target, which was intentionally placed so that they could appreciate the effect of the shots." At sunset they went away looking very grave, and talking earnestly. Fitz-Roy wondered if "our exercise might have frightened them more than I wished." Then he reassured himself that it may "have induced them to leave the place... without some such a demonstration they might have obliged us to fire on them instead of the target."[143]

It seems likely to me that practice-shooting took place in this evening (the 26th) while it was still light, before the serious incident of the old men (see below), even though Fitz-Roy stated that he organized the shooting demonstration as a "consequence" of this incident." The latter "incident" occurred "after dark," well after mid-night, and the shooting had to be presented while there was still daylight.

21. THE OLD MEN ARE NOT SO FRIENDLY

About an hour after dark (either January 26 or perhaps the 25th), the sentry on duty noticed a moving body. Thinking it was a wild animal, he was about to shoot at it when he realized it was a man. The suspect immediately dashed away and Fitz-Roy, who was awakened, thought he might have been planning "to surprise us, if asleep, [or] perhaps only to steal." Later he and Darwin were informed: two or three old men had attempted to force their way into a tent when they were halted by the sentry and motioned to keep away. One of the aggressors spat in the sentry's face, went off in a violent passion, muttering to himself, turning around several times making faces and angry gestures at the sentry. Darwin, who did not witnessed the incident either, added details, which he learned the following day.

The old man being told not to come so close, spat in the seamans face & then retreating behind the trench, made motions, which it was said, could mean nothing but skinning & cutting up a man. He acted it over a Fuegian, who was asleep & eyed at the same time our man, as much to say, this is the way I should like to serve you.[144]

If Darwin account is truer than imagined it shows a degree of hostility towards Fitz-Roy and company, far greater than I, and probably the reader, could have imagined.

22. DARWIN AND FITZ-ROY ARE ANXIOUS THE DAY BEFORE DEPARTURE: JANUARY 27

While the crew was finishing the last wigwam and planting the remaining vegetable seeds, Fitz-Roy was surprised to see all the canoes departing. Of the 120 or 300 visitors (peaceful neighbors and "bad" strangers), less than a half dozen remained. Darwin was also apprehensive.

Suddenly every woman and child & nearly all the men removed themselves & we were watching from a neighbouring hill. We were all very uneasy at this, as neither Jemmy nor York understood what it meant & it did not promise peace for the establishment... We were quite at loss to account for it."

Jemmy was even more perplexed because his family had also left. Fitz-Roy wondered if the strangers had gone to prepare an attack and for this reason had taken their women and children along. He and Darwin probably asked each other whether or not they had been impressed by the display of firearms and had feared that they would be shot at. Some of the sailors suspected that they intended to make a secret attack to steal the expedition's property, because they were furious that the sentry had offended the old man who spat on him.[145]

Fear of an attack by the "Yapoos" would explain why Jemmy's family had departed so rapidly the day before (the 26th). But if this were the case, why hadn't they informed Jemmy their reason for leaving? Jemmy told Fitz-Roy that his family had simply said they were going fishing and would return that night (the 26th), but they had not yet returned. By late morning (the 27th) Fitz-Roy was convinced that no attack would occur. York and Jemmy were also sure that they incurred no risk from those "Yapoos". But why had they all departed at once, in such a hurry? No one knew for sure.

Matthews said he would pass his first night, the 27th, on land, alone among the Fuegians. He seemed steady "in his honest intention to do good." Darwin wondered.

> Matthews, with his usual quiet fortitude (remarkable in a man apparently possessing little energy of character), determined to stay with the Fuegians, who evinced no alarm for themselves; and so we left them to pass their first awful night.[146]

Darwin thought it very doubtful that Matthews was "qualified for so arduous an undertaking [as a missionary in Wulaia]." As Matthews was to spend his first night in Wulaia, Fitz-Roy and the others rowed away, as usual, to sleep in the caravan boats, about a mile from the shore.[147]

23. THE LAST MORNING IN WULAIA, FOR NOW

They were relieved to find quiet upon their return, the morning of the 28th. The resident natives were behaving in a most friendly manner, some were spearing fish from their canoes. Matthews' resolve had not dampened. Jemmy informed the captain that friends had arrived at dawn, that his family would return soon and that the "bad men," the Yapoos, had gone back to their own country. Now everyone agreed that they had left in such a hurry, probably fearing that the crew might attack them with the firearms that had been demonstrated. The work in the gardens continued for a while and there were no more disturbing incidents.[148]

Fitz-Roy was also reassured because, during this week, nothing of any real consequence had been stolen, even the last two or three days when so many natives had been around. Jemmy had a knife picked out of his pocket by one native while another was talking to him and wary York had been robbed. Fuegia had not lost a thing. Fitz-Roy observed, as Darwin had, that the "kindness to her was remarkable and among the women she was quite a pet."[149]

24. FITZ-ROY INVITES DARWIN TO SAIL DOWN "GLACIER LANE": JANUARY 28...

Fitz-Roy sent the yawl and a whaleboat, with most of the crew, back to the *Beagle* waiting in Goree Road and decided to take the other two whaleboats to complete the survey of the Northwest Arm ("Glacier Lane") he had begun in May 1830, during the first voyage. Darwin commented that he had "most kindly allowed me to accompany him." One whaleboat would be under Fitz-Roy's command and the other assigned to Lieutenant Hamond. Matthews was still determined to stay on in Wulaia with his three Fuegian friends. So he was no worry. Ten days should suffice for him to make up his mind whether or not he wanted to remain there as a missionary.

About mid-day January 28, they set out, passed through Murray Narrows and veered west (to the left) into Beagle Channel, carried along by a fresh easterly wind. Darwin was pleased. "The day to our astonishment was over-poweringly hot, so that our skins were scorched: with this beautiful weather, the view in the middle of the Beagle Channel was very remarkable." They moved up the channel among huge whales swimming all about the ship, spouting in different directions. He saw "two of these monsters, probably male and female, slowly swimming one after the other, within less than a stone's throw of the shore..." As he wrote this text later, these whales reminded him of the day they had seen several spermaceti (sperm) whales leaping almost entirely out of the water (see chapter 5, below).[150] There were still some whales in the channel, which the commercial fishers had missed.

That night several "unwelcome canoes" approached them, as they were setting up their two tents on the shore of Isla Grande. Fitz-Roy was very put out and gave orders to embark immediately. They folded up their tents, picked up their half-cooked supper and off they went. "Twelve armed men, therefore, gave way to six unarmed, naked savages, and went on to another cove, where these annoying, because ignorant natives could not see us."[151] Darwin was also wary of these "barbarians," who despite being inferior in number might "dash your brains out with a stone" with the courage of a wild beast. They located a quiet, hopefully secluded, spot nearby, before midnight. While Fitz-Roy and the crew were preparing to sleep in the tents, Darwin spread his blanket-bag on the nearby shore of pebbles, as it was his turn to serve as the sentry. Alone in the silent night, he meditated:

> It was my watch till one oclock [sic]; there is something very solemn in such scenes, the consciousness rushes on the mind in how remote a corner of the globe you are then in; all tends to this end, the quiet of the night is interrupted only by the heavy breathing of the men, and the cry of night-birds – the occasional bark of a dog reminds one that the Fuegians may be prowling, close to the tents, ready for a fatal rush.[152]

The next day they reached Devil's Island, so named by Fitz-Roy in May 1830, because one of his crew had been so frightened by an owl, that he imagined was the devil in person staring at him.

Having camped that night, on the nearby Isla Grande undisturbed (probably at a place now called Yamana Point - Punta Yamana). Early the following morning they entered the Northwest Arm, where deep fjords and large glaciers (they are smaller now) descend to the north shore of this mile-wide channel, most of them directly into the water. Darwin was enthralled:

> The scenery here becomes eve grander than ore. The lofty mountains on the north side compose the granite axis, or backbone of the country, and boldly rise to a height of between three and four thousand feet, with one peak above six thousand feet
> They are covered by a wide mantle of perpetual snow, and numerous cascades pour their waters, through the woods, into the narrow channel below. In many parts, magnificent glaciers extend from the mountain side to the water's

edge. It is scarcely possible to imagine anything more beautiful than the beryl-like blue of these glaciers, and especially as contrasted with the dead white of the upper expanse of snow.[153]

The glaciers also fascinated Fitz-Roy.

Wherever these enormous glaciers were seen, we remarked the most beautiful light blue or sea green tints in portions of solid ice, caused by varied transmission, or reflection of light. Blue was the prevailing colour, and the contrast which its extremely delicate hue, with the dazzling white of other ice, afforded to the dark green foliage, the almost black precipices, and the deep, indigo blue water, was very remarkable.[154]

Why Fitz-Roy later named these "lofty mountains" after Darwin is explained below. He observed that they appear higher than they really are because they rise so abruptly from the shore. This enormous range extends along this entire "arm" for thirty miles from the large bay called Yendegalia (west of Ushwaia) to the very tip of Isla Grande, at Brecknock Peninsula. As if foreseeing a coming event Darwin exclaimed: "The fragments which had fallen from the glacier into the water, were floating away, and the channel with its icebergs presented, for the space of a mile, a miniature likeness of the Polar Sea."[155]

25. THE HERO OF THE DAY

Following this expression of wonder, the men hauled the two boats on shore about 200 yards from a glacier. While seated quietly around a fire preparing a hasty meal, they were suddenly shaken by a thundering noise. Looking up they saw a thick slice of the glacier crashing into the water and huge waves surging. The sound echoed in every direction as the great waves rolled towards them, threatening to sweep away the two boats or dash them to pieces. An instant later the boats were lifted high and tossed back and forth near the shore. Several men dashed to retrieve them. Darwin noted: "One of the seamen just caught hold of the bows, as the curling breaker reached it [them, the boats]: he was knocked over and over, but not hurt and had saved the boats." Had the force of the tidal waves destroyed the boats, they would have been stranded a hundred miles from nowhere, without provisions and no one in sight. Following this near catastrophe, they quickly pulled the boats back into the "Arm" and set out in search of another shore where they could finish lunch "very far from any glacier." Later Fitz-Roy clarified that the "one seaman" Darwin mentioned who saved the boats was Darwin himself, the hero of the day.[156]

26. DARWIN ON THE MAP

The next day, January 30, they emerged from the Northwest Arm into a sound, beyond Gordon Island (which divides the flow of the water and forms the north and south "arms"). Fitz-Roy named the "lofty mountains, "this sound, and an island in the middle of the sound after Darwin, because he had "so willingly encountered the discomfort and risk of a long cruise in a small loaded boat." Darwin was not very complimentary about "his sound," among "many unknown desolate islands." Besides, the weather that day was "wretchedly bad." He was consoled with a thought: "It was a great comfort finding all the natives absent." They finally found a "miserable" place, on a large boulder, to pitch their two tents. They tried to sleep surrounded by putrefying seaweed "and when the tide rose, we had to get up and move our blanket-bags."

Fitz-Roy had honored the budding naturalist by three names near the glacial area, as just mentioned. If he could have seen into the future, when *On the Origin of Species…* was published (in 1859), he might have thought three times before putting these "Darwins" on the map for eternity.

Still proceeding westward, along the large indented island called Londonderry also by Fitz-Roy, they entered Whaleboat Sound, named in memory of his stolen whaleboat whose ghost may have been haunting him as he glanced from one coast to the other. Again the reference is to 1830, the first Beagle voyage. By now, early February 1833, they had surveyed this sound as far as Stewart (also spelt Stuart) Island where Fitz-Roy ordered his men to turn the two boats back and return to Wulaia.

On February 3 they entered the Southwest Arm, which extends for thirty-two miles between Gordon and Hoste islands. This "arm" excited little interest perhaps because it lacks the breathtaking glaciers of its counterpart. The surveys here were done in a hasty manner because, as Fitz-Roy explained, "these shores, at present [are] almost useless to civilized man." Darwin checked off the return voyage in a few sentences, noting that having gone as far west as Stewart Island, about 150 miles, from where the *Beagle* was waiting (in Goree Road), they proceeded "with no adventure, back to Ponsonby Sound."[157]

27. A NOT-SO-FRIENDLY ENCOUNTER

Darwin was mistaken; an "adventure" was waiting. After they emerged from the Southwest Arm, into Beagle Channel, the crew and the captain were not happy when they recognized the party of Tekeenica Yahgans whom they had managed to avoid the week before. These "bothersome natives" had crossed the channel and were in full view, on the shore of Hoste Island, painted red and white and adorned with goose feathers and down. As Fitz-Roy gazed at them, suddenly his dark mood brightened.

> One of their women was noticed by several among us as being far from ill-looking; her features were regular, and, excepting a deficiency of hair on the eyebrow and rather thick lips, the contour of her face was sufficiently good to have been mistaken for that of a handsome Gypsy.[158]

At this moment he lauded the "handsome Gypsy," though his comments about the "south-eastern Tekeenica," Yahgans in the Cape Horn vicinity, were different.

Anyone may publish an unpleasant impression of other people but insult is not justified, in my opinion. Sixty pages before he characterized those Yahgans as "low in stature, ill-looking, and badly proportioned." The women's bodies were "largely out of proportion to their height; their features, especially those of the old, are scarcely less disagreeable than the repulsive ones of the men." Here are the worst insults.

About four feet and some inches is the stature of these she-Fuegians - by courtesy called women. They never walk upright: a stooping posture, and awkward movement, is their natural gait. They may be fit mates for such uncouth men; but to civilised people their appearance is disgusting. Very few exceptions were noticed.

Nor were the "uncouth" Tekeenica men spared: "Sometimes these satires upon mankind wear a part of the skin of a guanaco or a seal-skin upon their backs..."[159] This is strange verbal behavior for a gentleman of his Christian convictions and pride. Darwin never sank to this level of contempt.

On this February 5 (1833) Fitz-Roy's and the crew's attention became glued on the "handsome Gypsy," not because she was "far from ill-looking," but because she was wearing a loose linen garment that had been given to Fuegia Basket. Tension mounted when they also noticed that her companions were sporting bits of ribbon and scraps of red cloth that must also have belonged to Fuegia, or to Jemmy, or to York or perhaps to Matthews. Moreover, their air of "almost defiance" prompted Fitz-Roy to suspect that his protégés or Matthews had been harmed.[160] Enough was enough. They hurried on, back as quickly as possible to Wulaia.

When darkness set in they camped along the coast. At daybreak, while hastening through Murray Narrows, they sighted several natives wearing strips of tartan cloth and white linen "which we well knew were obtained from our poor friends." Without stopping to inquire, they pulled along with greater speed. Soon they would discover what had or had not happened during their ten days absence.

28. GOOD TIDINGS IN WULAIA: FEBRUARY 6

Closing in on Wulaia at noon, they sighted natives painted profusely and adorned with rags of English clothing. Fitz-Roy was again struck: these rags might be the last remnants of "our friends' stock." However, when the two boats touched shore, they recognized those who were greeting them as usual "hallooing and jumping about..." as the same who had been there ten days before. Matthews appeared, also as usual, much to Fitz-Roy's "extreme relief." Presently Jemmy and York came, looking well and Fuegia was safe in her wigwam. The worst fears, suspicions and secret accusations were swallowed whole, and the anguish expelled with sighs of relief.

The worst had not happened but Fitz-Roy sensed that something had. He took Matthews on board his whaleboat and moved it a short distance from the shore "to be free from interruption." Jemmy went on board the other whaleboat, while York waited on the beach. The local men were "squatted down on their hams to watch our proceedings, reminding me [Fitz-Roy] of a pack of hounds waiting for a fox to be unearthed." Matthews told him what had occurred during these ten days.

> He did not think himself safe, among such a set of utter savages as he found them to be, notwithstanding Jemmy's assurances to the contrary. No violence had been committed beyond holding down his head by force, as if in contempt of his strength; but he had been harshly threatened by several men, and from the signs used by them, he felt convinced they would take his life.[161]

29. THE "BAD MEN" HAD COME

Matthews also told Fitz-Roy "three days after our departure several canoes full of strangers to Jemmy's family arrived, and from that time on Matthews had had no peace by day, and very little rest at night." These strangers "tried to tire him out by making an incessant noise close to his head." An old man had threatened to kill him with a large stone if he didn't give him what was demanded. Once a "whole party came armed with stones and stakes and if he had nothing to give them, teased him by pulling the hair on his face." Darwin heard that "some of the younger men and Jemmy's brother were crying" but couldn't stop them. Matthews had managed to quiet them with presents. Darwin concluded: "I think we arrived just in time to save his life." It was probably then that Matthews informed Fitz-Roy that he had made up his mind not to attempt to convert such "savages".

Fitz-Roy learned that Matthews "only partisans" were the women who had always received him kindly, made room for him by the fire, and shared their food with him without asking for anything. Jemmy had guarded his wigwam when he went visiting the women. But these visits ceased after the first three days when the "strangers" appeared. From that time on the strangers, and even some of the local men, were "engrossed by the tools, clothes and crockery ware" in his wigwam, though his most valuable possessions had not been discovered, hidden as they were under the floor and in the apex of his wigwam. Darwin reported that the clothes that were stolen had been torn up and divided among them (a Yahgan, not an Oens-men custom).

York and Fuegia had not lost a thing "but Jemmy was sadly plundered, even by his own family." The gardens had been "trampled over repeatedly" despite Jemmy's efforts to shield them. He looked very sorrowful as he slowly shook his head saying: "My people very bad; great fool[s]; know nothing at all very great fool[s]." Then as he told Darwin that his own brother (not named) had stolen many things from him, he exclaimed "what fashion call that" [no question mark]…He abused his countrymen, 'all bad men, no sabe (know) nothing,' and though I never hear him swear before [Jemmy added] 'dammed fools.'" He looked so disconsolate that Darwin was sure that at that time he would "have been glad to have returned [to England] with us."[162] It is evident that strangers were the "bad men," the neighbors, the same who had come on 26 January. Once they knew that Fitz-Roy and his crew had departed, they returned to Wulaia to rob Matthews.

30. DEPARTURE FROM WULAIA, FOR NOW; DARWIN HAS A SECOND THOUGHT

Fitz-Roy informed Matthews and the others that all of them were to precede the following day (February 7) back to the *Beagle*, waiting in Goree Road. But how to get his property from his wigwam, into the whaleboats "in the face of a hundred Fuegians?" Despite Fitz-Roy's worries, the task was accomplished expeditiously. When the last bundles were being carried to the boats, no disturbing incident had occurred. Fitz-Roy was grateful and distributed axes, saws, gimlets, knives and nails among the helpers. He said good-bye to his three protégés and to the "wondering throng assembled on the beach," promising he would return several days later with a few men.[163]

Darwin and most of the crew bade farewell to their three friends. He was sorry to leave them though he probably knew he would see them again. The following is quoted from his diary, which he altered significantly for publication.

> It was quite melancholy leaving our Fuegians amongst their barbarous countrymen: there was one comfort; they appeared to have no personal fears.
>
> But in contradiction of what has often been stated, 3 years has been sufficient to change savages, into, as far as habits go, complete & voluntary Europeans. *York, who was a full grown man & with a strong violent mind, will I am certain in every respect live as far as his means go, like an Englishman.* Poor Jemmy, looked rather disconsolate, & certainly would have liked to have returned with us; he said 'they were all very bad men, no sabe nothing'…
>
> I am afraid whatever other ends their excursion to England produces, it will not be conductive to their happiness. *They have far too much sense not to see the vast superiority of civilized over uncivilized habits; & yet I am afraid to the latter they must return.*[164]

He modified the parts of his diary, (indicated above in italics), four or five years later, when he wrote the text for volume 3 of the *Narrative…* (published later as *The Voyage of the Beagle*). Then he had second thoughts, he realized that York would never live "like an Englishman." Also, he ended his published text (in chapter ten of *The Voyage…*) more emphatically, than in his diary. "I fear it is more than doubtful, whether their visit [to England] will have been of any use to them."[165]

On February 7, they boarded the two whaleboats and rowed back to Goree Road via the southern route through Nassau Bay. They reached the *Beagle* before dark, despite the rough sea. They had covered a total of 300 miles in the open boats from January 19 to February 7. Meanwhile, the *Beagle* had been refitted and was ready for her next assignment.[166] The entire crew was reunited in Goree Road for three days and on February 10 the *Beagle*, with all the men and boats, sailed back across Nassau Bay to Packsaddle Bay near Orange Bay, Hoste Island.

31. FITZ-ROY RETURNS TO WULAIA WITHOUT DARWIN: FEBRUARY 14

Fitz-Roy and a few men left the *Beagle* in Packsaddle Bay and returned to Wulaia in a whaleboat or the yawl. During three days they navigated slowly through Ponsonby Sound, went on land at times to explore the east coast of Hoste, sighted natives but "had little intercourse with them." Approaching Wulaia, the morning of February 14, Fitz-Roy was relieved to see the women fishing quietly from their canoes and thought that this scene augured well for peace. When they went ashore they found York busy building a canoe out of the planks left for him by the caravan. Jemmy was also making a canoe, by hollowing out the trunk of a large tree as he had seen done in Río de Janeiro on the return voyage. (These were probably the first plank and dugout canoes in the area.) Fuegia was neatly dressed. She and York still had their possessions: only Jemmy had been robbed again. His mother came to greet Fitz-Roy also "decently clothed." Even vegetables were sprouting in the gardens.[167]

32. MEANWHILE, THE "STRANGERS"

The only distressing news was that "strangers" had returned on February 8, the day after Fitz-Roy and the others had departed. This time Jemmy and his people had "very much jaw" with them and fought them using stone missiles. The enemy kidnapped ("stole") two women and Jemmy's party, one of their women. Jemmy assured Fitz-Roy that they had been driven away and that now he was getting along fine.

Fitz-Roy departed still hoping that his protégés would effect some positive changes among their countrymen and that upon his return (a year later), Matthews might be persuaded to remain among them.[168] Just who these strangers were was not stated. They were probably the same Beagle Channel "bad" Yahgan neighbors who had attacked Matthews two weeks earlier. If they had been the Oens-men, Jemmy would have been much more alarmed.

33. FIRST DEPARTURE FROM TIERRA DEL FUEGO: LATE FEBRUARY 1833

Fitz-Roy joined the rest of the crew waiting in Packsaddle Bay, near Orange Bay (Hoste Island) on February 15. Darwin briefly mentioned two excursions he made on foot, across southern Hoste to survey its west coast. He remarked on the views from the hilltops and the beautiful weather.[169]

About February 17 the *Beagle* weighed anchor and the following few days the crew surveyed the northern section of Wollaston Island but saw no natives. Then the *Beagle* returned to the "old quiet place in Goree Road" and the next day they headed towards Le Maire Strait and Good Success Bay. Fitz-Roy reported that "the night of the 22nd was one of the most stormy I ever witnessed." The wind was so furious in Good Success Bay that the crew feared they would be driven out, back into the strait. Even when the wind calmed down the surf was so strong that they had difficulty landing the boats on the shore of the bay. The local natives (the Haush) did not appear during their entire stay. Darwin and others climbed Bank's Hill, as they had in December 1832, but confronted such strong winds and cold that they beat a hasty retreat back to the ship. Darwin was surprised to see that their footprints (bootprints) had not been effaced during the nine weeks, since they had been there, and that they could even identify them (just like the Haush and Selk'nam could their prints). The crew spent most of the five days in the bay on board fishing for skate and codfish, which were delicious. They "put to sea" from Good Success, on February 26, sailing through a "most disagreeable swell off Cape San Diego," and then ran before another gale, hoping to make the Falkland Islands safely and soon.

34. ELSEWHERE, THE FOLLOWING ELEVEN MONTHS: EARLY MARCH 1833 TO LATE JANUARY 1834

This period is merely summarized because the narration begins again on January 26, 1834 when the *Beagle* entered Magellan Strait.

The crew spent the entire month of March to April 6, 1833 on East Falkland Island. Both Fitz-Roy and Darwin were very much aware of the British "take over" of the Falkland Islands, from the Argentine

Republic. On January 2, 1833 two British warships had arrived, had hoisted the Union Jack, forced the small Argentine garrison to evacuate the islands and named them Falkland in honor of the Viscount Falkland, a British naval officer, who in 1690, as a member of a British expedition, made the first clearly recorded landing there. The British claim is derived from Falkland's report. The islands had been called Malvinas, as they are still known today in Argentina. This name is derived from Malouines, used by fishermen from the port of Saint Malo, Bretagne (France), who were the first Europeans to take advantage of its strategic location for the fisheries and established a base there when it was still uninhabited, probably during the mid-eighteenth century.

During this first visit Fitz-Roy purchased a sealing schooner from William Low, the Scottish sealing master. Later Fitz-Roy named the schooner *Adventure* and appointed Wickham as her captain. The next year, in February 1834, he hired Low as the pilot of his former vessel. Thus Darwin became acquainted with Low and heard his stories about cannibalism from Bob, and the account of the "whale feast" referred to in the last chapter.

During the following nine months, from early April 1833 to late January 1834, while Fitz-Roy surveyed the coasts of Uruguay and Argentina, Darwin made important excursions on horseback. He was observing, taking notes, and collecting specimens as never before and sending the specimens all back to Professor Henslow, manly from Montevideo. He was often exuberant, ill only once and wrote numerous letters home.

In Uruguay, late April to June (1833), and in July again he rode on horseback for days on end through the backcountry of Maldonado. Mid-August he was back in Argentina. He rode from the delta of Rio Negro, near a fort called Carmen de Patagones (northern Patagonia), to a nearby garrison along the Colorado River, the headquarters of General Juan Manuel Rosas, Argentina's most powerful military and political figure, who was exterminating and subduing the Pampa Indians. From September 8 to 20, again on horseback, Darwin traversed the recently pacified region from Rio Colorado to Buenos Aires, with a military escort given to him by General Rosas. From there he continued on to Santa Fe. In early October he became ill with a fever there and took a boat, down the Parana River, back to Buenos Aires. After some delays, he crossed the La Plata Estuary to Montevideo. In November, while waiting to meet the *Beagle*, he rode horseback far into the countryside,

Anne Chapman

for several weeks, beyond the inland town of Mercedes (Uruguay), and found other important fossils, in addition to those he had discovered near Bahia Blanca (Argentina) in September and October of 1832.

The last week of December 1833 Fitz-Roy began surveying the Atlantic coast of Patagonia and late January 1834 he turned the *Beagle* into the Magellan Strait.[170]

CHAPTER 5

DARWIN'S LAST VISITS
IN TIERRA DEL FUEGO: 1834

1. HE ENTERS MAGELLAN STRAIT AND MEETS
THE TEHUELCHE INDIANS: JANUARY 26-30

A few days later the *Beagle* was beyond the First Narrows, sailing against strong westerly gales with tides rising forty to fifty feet, running five and six miles per hour. Darwin thought of his illustrious predecessors, Ferdinand Magellan and Francis Drake. "Who can wonder at the dread of the early navigators of these Straits?"

He was introduced to a tribe of "Patagonians" (Tehuelches), near their *toldos* (large shelters of guanaco or horse skins) in Gregory Bay on the continental shore of the strait. Among them was María, whom Darwin called Santa María. Captain King had met her when he entered the strait in September 1827 and Fitz-Roy in 1829, during the first voyage. She and her companions had frequent contacts with navigators and sealers so they spoke some English and Spanish. Darwin thought they were "half civilized and proportionally demoralized," also "rather wild." The men, about six feet tall, clothed in mantles of guanaco hides, their long black hair streaming about their painted faces, impressed Darwin. But he noticed they rode astride horses that were too small for their heavy loads. He thought they resembled "the Indians with General Rosas," the Pampa Indians whom he had seen the year before in

August, though they were much more painted, "many with their whole faces red, & brought to a point on the chin, others black. One man was ringed & dotted with white like a Fuegian."

The Patagonians apparently liked these Europeans. When Fitz-Roy invited three to come on board "everyone seemed determined to be one of them." Darwin added: "At tea they [the privileged three] behaved quite like gentlemen used a knife & fork & helped themselves with a spoon. Nothing was so much relished as Sugar." As they were not canoe people, like the Yamana and Alakaluf, when they felt the ship tipping back and forth they were eager to return on land.

The next day the "whole population of the Toldos" promptly lined up on the bank anxious to barter their guanaco skins and ostrich (rhea) feathers, for firearms. Being denied the latter, they accepted tobacco but not the knives and axes they were offered. Darwin found it impossible not to like "these mis-named giants, they were so thoroughly good-humoured and unsuspecting."[171] Fitz-Roy had a different impression of this encounter. "They received us kindly, but...two men standing up in the midst of them, who looked immoveably grave and stupidly dignified...An active barter commenced, but the portly actors in the middle did not take part in it, they remained in their solemnity till we left them."[172]

Maria greeted one of the *Beagle* crew she had met a year and a half earlier at Rio Negro. She and her tribe had ridden on horseback from the shore of the Magellan Strait, Gregory Bay, to Rio Negro, some 800 miles (1482 km), to trade their guanaco skins and rhea feathers, probably for firearms and tobacco.[173] This was quite a trek for families with their babies and heavy tents, fording deep rivers and riding through long stretches of the dry, wind-swept plains of Patagonia, though they had spare horses to ride and to eat. Darwin was aware of the vital importance of the horse, that had so radically transformed the lives of the Patagonians (Tehuelches).

Thinking of their horses, Darwin noted:

> This is a very curious fact, showing the extraordinarily rapid multiplication of horses in South America. The horse was first landed at Buenos Aires in 1537, and the colony being then for a long time deserted, the horse ran wild and

in 1580, only forty-three years afterwards, we hear of them
at the Strait of Magellan![174]

2. DARWIN'S "ADVENTURE" NEAR PORT FAMINE: FEBRUARY 2 TO 10

The *Beagle* anchored in Port Famine, the base used during the first
Beagle voyage, about the center of the strait. That day (February 2)
they sighted, at a distance of ninety miles, the highest mountain in Tierra del Fuego, Mount Sarmiento (6,800 feet). A few days later Darwin
ventured to climb a nearer, smaller mountain, the Tarn (some 2600
feet). He and his companions crawled up the mountain, through
gloomy, cold, wet terrain of decaying, moldering trunks, sinking knee
deep into the boggy rotten terrain. During a pause Darwin glanced
down at the deep ravines, a "death-like scene of desolation." They had
almost given up hope or desire to reach the summit when they climbed
on a bare ridge where Darwin viewed the landscape, through the piercing cold wind and fog and felt somewhat rewarded. "Here was a true
Tierra del Fuego view; irregular chains of hills, mottled with patches of
snow, deep yellowish-green valleys, & arms of the sea running in all
directions." Moreover, he found some fossil shells.

The next day the Port Famine weather became "splendidly
clear,"and he longed for more of the same. "If Tierra del [Fuego] could
boast one such day a week, she would not be so thoroughly detested as
she is by all who know her."[175] He did not appreciate Fuegian weather.

3. BACK THROUGH THE MAGELLAN STRAIT; DARWIN SIGHTS THE OENS-MEN: FEBRUARY 10 –13

Fitz-Roy, and the entire crew boarded the *Beagle* to make a rapid
survey of the Atlantic coast of Isla Grande. Two days later, still in the
strait, Darwin sighted the "Ohens-men" (the Selk'nam) on Elizabeth
Island (Isabel in Spanish).

During the day we passed close to Elizabeth Island, on the
North end of which there was a party of Fuegians with

their canoe &c. They were tall men & clothed in mantles;
& belong probably to the East Coast [Isla Grande]; the
same set of men we saw in Good Success Bay; they are
clearly different from the Fuegians, & ought to be called
foot Patagonians. Jemmy Button had a great horror of
these men, under the name of Ohens men.

But how could these "Ohens men" be on an island if they were not
navigators? Here Darwin's confusion may be explained by assuming
that the "party of Fuegians," were a mixed group: Alakalufs with their
canoe and a few "foot Patagonians," the tall men with mantles, Jemmy's
Oens-men, who lived nearby on the Isla Grande. Darwin saw the latter
from a distance and may have only noticed the tallest men, whom he
realized were physically similar to the Haush he had met in Good Success Bay in December 1832. The Alakaluf inhabited the central and
western sections on the continental shore of the strait, while the Oens-
men lived along the opposite shore (Isla Grande). The latter, cited by
Darwin as "the foot Patagonians," had probably gotten a ride to Elizabeth Island with the Alakaluf.[176]

Darwin and the others did not go ashore on Elizabeth island but they
did in nearby Gregory Bay, the next morning, to obtain guanaco meat
(again from the Teheulches). He greeted their "friends the Indians
[who] anxiously seemed to desire our Presence." Among them was a
mestizo from Montevideo who had been with them for four years, and
"two boat Indians" (Alakaluf) who, as Darwin noticed, spoke a different
language, not similar to the Patagonians (the Tehuelches).[177]

4. WHALES OFF THE NORTH COAST OF ISLA GRANDE: FEBRUARY 14- 21

During the following week Fitz-Roy completed his survey of a section of the Atlantic coast of Isla Grande to San Sebastian Bay. Darwin
admired the large numbers of Spermaceti (Sperm) whales in this bay.

In 1972 I walked among their bones that were scattered along its
shore. When I returned there a few years later all the bones had disap-
peared, carried away perhaps by scientists and other whalebone fans.

17. I am seated on the vertebrae possibly of a sperm whale, San Sebastian Bay, 1972.

5. DARWIN ADMIRES "FINE TALL MEN..." IN THETIS BAY: LATE FEBRUARY 1834

Continuing down the coast of Isla Grande, they stopped over in Thetis Bay near the entrance to Le Maire Strait where they met "foot Patagonians, fine tall men with Guanaco mantles." As this was Haush territory, they were probably the same group, though not the same men, Darwin had met in Good Success Bay. This time he admired these "fine tall men...[who] with nothing more than their slight arrows, manage to kill such strong wary animals [guanacos]."[178]

6. THE WOLLASTON ISLANDERS, THE MOST "MISERABLE" OF ALL THE FUEGIANS

Having navigated the "uncomfortable Strait," (Le Maire) they crossed Nassau Bay and circled down towards Cape Horn, to Wollaston Island. On the evening of February 24 the *Beagle* anchored "under Wollaston." The next day as they were going ashore "near Wollaston Island, we pulled along side a canoe with six Fuegians." That day he went on the island, saw a wigwam and "crawled" to the top of the nearby hills where he inspected the soil and viewed the area. The last full day there, February 26, the weather was very stormy so they stayed on board and the next day headed for Beagle Channel and Jemmy's territory.[179]

Recall that I quoted Darwin's remarks above, as his first "meditation," about the scenes of the Wollaston island natives he witnessed, now on February 25 and 26 (1834). The vision of these "poor wretches," the most "miserable creatures" he ever beheld, together with the image of other Fuegians (also Yahgans) devouring their old women seem to have convinced him that all the Fuegians were utter savages despite his amusing, though sometimes exasperating, encounters with other Yahgans and his fondness for Jemmy Button (see below).

18. Scene of the 1969 expedition, near Thetis Bay, one of the guides and myself, taken by Domingo Palma.

7. AMUSING CONTACTS
ON THE WAY BACK TO WULAIA

Sailing from Wollaston they crossed Nassau Bay again, passed through Goree Road, going north towards Beagle Channel. They found a "beautiful little cove" near the northeast corner of Navarin Island, probably close to where they had been in January 1833 in the caravan. The first day of March, they met three canoes full of "Yapoo Tekeenica [Yahgans] who were very quiet & civil & more amusing than any Monkeys." Darwin was served two fish on the point of a spear when he handed a large nail to one of the men and noticed again that when a present landed in the wrong canoe, the recipients passed it on to the canoe for which it was intended.[180]

On March 2, they were "beating against the Westerly winds" along Beagle Channel, and two uneventful days later reached the "Northern part of Ponsonby sound," meaning the entrance to Murray Narrows, probably Lewaia, where they spent the entire day. It was here or near here, the year before, that Jemmy told his stories about the Oens-men. Now, on March 4, 1834, ten or twelve canoes paddled alongside the *Beagle*, full of natives anxious to barter fish and crabs "for bits of cloth & rags." A handsome young woman, whose face was painted black, smiled with satisfaction as she tied bits of the "gay rags" round her head. Her husband "enjoyed the very universal privilege in this country of possessing two wives." He was obviously jealous of the attention paid to his smiling wife, when he ordered "his naked beauties" to paddle away.

Having camped there, the next morning they headed down Murray Narrows for Wulaia. While the *Beagle* zigzagged through the narrows, tacking to take advantage of the changing wind, the men in the canoes paddled with all their might to keep up with her. Darwin was delighted.

> The natives did not at all understand the reason of our tacking, and, instead of meeting us at each tack, vainly strove to follow us in our zig-zag course. The more Fuegians the merrier; and very merry work it was. Both parties laughing, wondering, gaping at each other; we pitying them, for giving us good fish and crabs for rags, &c; they

19. The *Beagle* in Murray Narrows: by Conrad Martens.

grasping at the chance of finding people so foolish as to exchange such splendid ornaments [and rags] for a good supper.[181]

Here he noticed what is often an essential quality of barter: an exchange of objects that have little value for the giving party but are highly valued by the receiving party.[182]

He was pleased by the difference it made "being quite superior in force" on the *Beagle* instead of on a whaleboat, as the previous year. He recalled how annoyed he had been by sound of the voices incessantly hollering *yammerschooner*. Now he was in a good mood, though flabbergasted that these Fuegians showed "so little interest in the many marvels of his ship" and that their admiration was excited far more by scarlet cloths or blue beads, by the seamen washing themselves and by the "absence of women."[183] Their fascination for red cloths and blue beads soon wore off, but not their awareness of the absence of women. Despite Darwin's formidable powers of observation, he was not attentive to what the natives probably thought of these lone male navigators. The lack of women must have struck the Yahgans as extremely odd. They were overjoyed when they met a captain's wife, Mrs. Snow, twenty-one years later, in 1855. She was perhaps the first white woman the Yahgans had seen in Tierra del Fuego.[184]

8. FAREWELL WULAIA: MARCH 5-6, 1834

Seven canoes trailed them through the narrows "this being a populous part of the country." The crew disembarked in Wulaia, anxious to learn how the three protégés had been making out during the year's absence, but not a soul was in sight. The wigwams built last year were deserted and the gardens trampled on. The sailors dug up a few turnips and potatoes that were served at the captain's table. After the meal, Fitz-Roy and others wandered about still without seeing anyone.[185]

An hour or so later, they sighted three canoes paddling towards them from Button Island. In one of them the Union Jack was flying high and a man was standing as if washing the paint off his face. Darwin recognized him.

This man was poor Jemmy, now a thin haggard savage, with long disordered hair, and naked, except a bit of a blanket round his waist. We did not recognise him till he was close to us, for he was ashamed of himself, and turned his back to the ship. We had left him plump, fat, clean and well dressed; I never saw so complete and grievous a change.

He recalled that Jemmy had been "so particular about his clothese [sic], that he was always afraid of even dirtying his shoes; scarcely ever without gloves & his hair neatly cut."

Fitz-Roy, using binoculars, distinguished two natives in the canoe washing their faces and recognized one as Tommy. When the other gave the sailor's greeting, Fitz-Roy knew he could only be Jemmy,

but, how altered! I could hardly restrain my feelings, and I was not, by any means, the only one so touched by his squalid miserable appearance. He was naked, like his companions, except a bit of skin about his loins; his hair was long and matted, just like theirs; he was wretchedly thin, and his eyes were affected by smoke.

Once on board, Fitz-Roy hurried him below to clothe him. Soon he was dining at the captain's table "using his knife and fork properly, and in every way behaving as correctly as if he had never left us." Nor had he forgotten his English. To the astonishment of the crew, his family spoke to Fitz-Roy in English, Jemmy's English.

He "recollected every one well, and was very glad to see them all, especially Mr. Bynoe and James Bennett." He gave Bynoe "a fine otter skin which he had dressed and kept purposely" and another to Bennett. Darwin noted in his diary: "Poor Jemmy with his usual good feeling brought two beautiful otter skins for his two old friends & some spear heads & arrows of his own making for the Captain."[186] When asked if he had been ill, he replied: "Hearty, sir, never better." He reassured them that he had "plenty fruits, plenty birdies, ten guanacos in snow time," and "too much fish."

Darwin wrote to his youngest sister, Catherine, a month later, that Jemmy "was quite contented", despite the fact that the year before "at

20. A Yahgan man who looks like Darwin's and Fitz-Roy's description of Jemmy when they met him for the last time on March 5, 1834: by Conrad Martens.

the height of his indignation, he said his country people no sabe nothing damned fools now they were very good people, with too much to eat & all the luxuries of life."[187]

9. JEMMY'S PREFERENCE

Darwin and Fitz-Roy "were rather surprised, to find he had not the least wish to return to England." In the same letter to Catherine, Darwin commented: "The Captain offered to take him to England, but this, to our surprise, he at once refused: in the evening his young wife came alongside & showed us the reason." Soon after the meal, a voice announced in English "Jemmy Button's wife." Fitz-Roy noticed "the reason," the good-looking young woman in Jemmy's canoe. The shawls, handkerchiefs, and the gold-laced cap she received, failed to calm her fears. She waited anxiously for the return of her spouse to the canoe. Tommy called to him in a loud voice; "Jemmy Button, canoe, come!" But she kept on crying until he appeared the deck. Finally they all departed in the three canoes laden with gifts, promising to return in the morning.

10. MATTHEWS' PREFERENCE

The next morning, following breakfast on board, Fitz-Roy and Matthews had a long conversation. Matthews had been on the *Beagle* the entire year and still expressed no desire to be left in Wulaia. Fitz-Roy then realized that such a job would be too much for him.[188]

11. YORK'S AND FUEGIA'S PREFERENCE

Jemmy told Fitz-Roy that York and Fuegia had returned to their own country some months before in the large plank canoe York had built. He said that they were very happy when they departed loaded with presents, however, adding "York very much jaw...pick up big stones...all men afraid."

Later Jemmy confided in Fitz-Roy and Darwin that York and Fuegia had escaped in their large canoe during an incursion of the Oens-men. Afterwards they returned and persuaded Jemmy and his family, including his mother, to accompany them "to look at his [York's] land." So they all went: York and Fuegia in their large canoe and the others in three canoes, up Murray Narrows to Devil's Island (near the entrance to the Northwest Arm in Beagle Channel). York's brother and their "Alikhoolip tribe" were waiting there for them. That night Fuegia, York and his "tribe" robbed Jemmy of nearly all his "things" while he was sleeping, leaving him totally naked and then they "stoled off", back to their own "country" (probably through the Northwest Arm).

Darwin remarked that York "appears to have treated Fuegia very ill." However, according to Fitz-Roy: "Fuegia seemed to be very happy, and quite contented with her lot." Jemmy asserted that she helped to "catch (steal) his clothes, while he was asleep, the night before York left him naked." Fitz-Roy was indignant at this "last act of that cunning fellow." Darwin called it "an act of consummate villainy." Now they fully realized that York had decided to stay in Wulaia calculating that he would obtain more presents there than had he been left in his own country, and that he had built a large canoe to transport "his ill-gotten gains."

12. THE OENS-MEN HAD ATTACKED

"The much dreaded Oens-men came in numbers," after Fitz-Roy had left Wulaia (February 14, 1833). Darwin identified them: "They clearly are the tall men, the foot Patagonians of the east coast." They were the Selk'nam, who inhabited the Atlantic coast of the Isla Grande. This entire coast is often called the east coast, because it borders the Atlantic Ocean, though in realty its direction is north.

When they appeared on the horizon Jemmy and his "tribe" fled to the small islands, taking all of their "valuables," all they managed to collect. The Oens-men carried off whatever remained in Wulaia. Fitz-Roy thought: "They had doubtless heard of the houses and property left there, and hastened to seize upon it – like other 'borderers' [the neighboring Yahgans, the 'bad men']." After this last depredation Jemmy went to live on "his own island" (Button) and since then had never returned because it was a safer there than Wulaia and had sufficient food.

Jemmy and Tommy strolled about with Bynoe pointing out where the tents had been pitched the year before and "where the boundary line was." Jemmy told him that he had watched the gardens "day after day for the sprouting of peas, beans, and other vegetables" but even so his countrymen trampled over them, despite his protests. The three large wigwams had been deserted after the first frosts because they were so high that they were too cold to inhabit during the winter.[189]

13. FITZ-ROY'S FAREWELL TO JEMMY

Fitz-Roy felt that Jemmy's family was pleased by his return from England and ready to cooperate with "men of other lands." The first step towards civilization had been taken. However, Jemmy was "but an individual, with limited means." The attempt to establish a mission with just three Fuegians was an illusion, "on too small a scale...[nonetheless] I cannot help still hoping that some benefit, however slight may result from the intercourse of these people, Jemmy, York, and Fuegia, with other natives of Tierra del Fuego. Perhaps a ship-wrecked seaman may hereafter receive help and kind treatment from Jemmy Button's children." Then Fitz-Roy wrote this homage to Jemmy.

> That Jemmy felt sincere gratitude is, I think, proved by his having so carefully preserved two fine otter skins, as I mentioned; by his asking me to carry a bow and quiver full of arrows to the schoolmaster of Walthamstow, with whom he had lived; by his having made two spear-heads expressly for Mr. Darwin; and by the pleasure he showed at seeing us all again.

The final moment of March 6, 1834, had arrived. Seeing Jemmy and his family in their canoes, ready to return home, Fitz-Roy appeared to be sad to leave them forever more.

> As nothing more could be done, we took leave of our young friend and his family, every one of whom was loaded with presents, and [we] sailed away from Woollya.[190]

14. DARWIN'S FAREWELL TO JEMMY

Every soul on board was heartily sorry to shake hands with him for the last time. I do not now doubt that he will be as happy as, perhaps happier than, if he had never left his own country. Everyone must sincerely hope that Captain Fitz Roy's noble hope may be fulfilled, of being rewarded for the many generous sacrifices which he made for these Fuegians, by some shipwrecked sailor being protected by the descendants of Jemmy Button and his tribe! When Jemmy reached the shore, he lighted a signal fire, and the smoke curled up, bidding us a last and long farewell, as the ship stood on her course into the open sea.[191]

And Loren Eiseley paid this homage to Darwin.

His account of Jemmy Button and the last signal fire lit by the latter in farewell to his white friends as the Beagle stood out to sea contains the pathos of great literature... Charles Darwin came close to envisaging the problem of culture as he bade good-by to his Indian shipmates. It is perhaps too much to expect of one man in an intellectually confused period that he should have solved both sides of the human mystery, or have distinguished clearly between the biological and the cultural. On that day in his youth, however, in a great surge of human feeling, he stood very close to doing so.[192]

15. THE EXPEDITION CARRIES ON

From Wulaia they sailed directly to East Falkland Island, arrived on March 10, for the second and last visit, where they remained until April 7. Then they proceeded to southern Patagonia, near the entrance to Magellan Strait. On April 18, they took three whaleboats up the Santa Cruz River to the foothills of the Andes and on May 7 arrived back to the *Beagle*, safe and sound. On May 16 they anchored off Cape Virgins

21. Jemmy and his family biding farewell to the *Beagle* crew, whom they will never see again: a section of a drawing by Conrad Martens.

at the very tip of the continental mass, at the entrance to the strait, where they spent almost two weeks "beating about the entrance to the strait, obtaining soundings."

Once in the strait, on May 29, they stopped over in Gregory Bay again but "our old friends the Indians were not there." Sailing towards Port Famine a few days later, they rescued two "worthless vagabonds" who had deserted a sealing ship and joined the Patagonians (Tehuelches). Darwin commented: "They had been treated by these Indians with their usual disinterested noble hospitality." The men had strayed from them and had been hiking along the coast for so many days that they were in a pitiful state when the *Beagle* crew sighted them "yet they were in good health."[193]

16. FAREWELL ALAKALUFS

The *Beagle* remained in Port Famine the first week of June (1834). Fitz-Roy noted that the Fuegians (Alakalufs) "twice came & plagued us. As there were many instruments, clothes, and men on shore, it was thought necessary to frighten them away." He ordered the crew to fire "a great gun" towards them from a distance. Darwin related:

> The first time a few great guns were fired, when they were far distant. It was most ludicrous to watch through a glass the Indians, as often as the shot struck the water, take up stones, and as a bold defiance, throw them towards the ship, though about a mile and a half distant![194]

Then Fitz-Roy sent a boat closer to them and ordered his men to fire musket balls near but not to aim to kill. Hiding behind trees, the Indians fired arrows, after every musket discharge, which always fell short of their boat. Darwin then related (in his diary) that "the officer pointed to them & laughing made the Fuegians frantic with rage (as they well might be at so unprovoked an attack); they shook their very mantles with passion." But when they saw the musket balls cutting through the trees, they fled in their canoes. Fitz-Roy chased them in his boat but soon desisted. Later another group approached the *Beagle* and was driven into a little stream. The next day Fitz-Roy sent two boats to drive them still further away. Darwin seemed even less amused.

> It was admirable to see the determination with which four or five men came forward to defend themselves against three times that number. As soon as they saw the boats they advanced a 100 yards towards us, prepared a barricade of rotten tress & busily picked up piles of stones for their slings. Every time a musket was pointed towards them, they in return pointed an arrow. I feel sure they would not have moved till more than one had been wounded. This being the case we retreated.[195]

Fitz-Roy and his crew, like other well-armed jokers (sealers and adventurers), taunted the Alakaluf, mocking their efforts to fend off attacks. Such was Fitz-Roy's and the *Beagle* crew's final farewell to the Fuegians.

17. THE "DESTINY" OF THE ALAKALUF

By 1900, the Alakaluf had been nearly "wiped out" by the diseases they caught from outsiders and addiction to the alcoholic drinks they were offered. The small groups that remained were piecing together their lives; working on the fishing boats of their Chilean neighbors, selling fish in the markets of port towns, especially Punta Arenas, and offering fish and baskets, from their canoes, to seamen and tourists in passing ships. Today (2006) a colony of Alakaluf, who preferred to be called Kaweskar, live in Puerto Eden, about the middle of the Pacific archipelago. Nine or ten still speak their language as well as Spanish, among whom several are college graduates as sophisticated as any anthropologist. They are determined to develop their Kaweskar identity, not to let it drown in the deep waters of the fjords.[196]

18. AND THE YAHGAN...

They had "survived" in Tierra del Fuego for at least six thousands years (according to the archaeologists), thanks to their ancestral cus-

22. This drawing showing Captain Joshua Slocum (from Cape Cod, New England), was published in his book. He was the first man to sail alone around the world in a small boat. Here, in 1896, he is shooting towards the Alakaluf in the Magellan Strait. A similar scene took place when the *Beagle* was leaving Magellan Strait though the crew didn't shoot to kill, neither did Slocum.

toms of sharing, their perfected technology (given the material available), and their "original" abundant marine resources though life had never been easy mainly because of the unpredictable, sometimes harsh, climate. Also mortal accidents in the canoes were probably always quite frequent and minor aliments, especially sore eyes from the fires in the huts. But they had a cheerful temperament, as the early navigators almost invariably observed, and had found life well worth living, as Darwin noted.[197]

Darwin was there before the missionaries arrived, and before the onslaught of the epidemics. A few years ago an outstanding Chilean historian, Mateo Martinic B, analyzed the impact of the Anglican missionaries (as of 1869 to 1917) on the Yahgan population and that of the colonization. The well-meaning missionaries imposed changes in the native "life style" that debilitated their ability to resist the coming epidemics and to confront other problems. The causes of the cultural and physical demise of the Yahgans are well known: first and foremost the epidemics brought unintentionally by the Europeans; plagues and sicknesses for which the natives had no natural defenses, as they had never been exposed to them previously. The first epidemic recorded occurred in 1863 when Jemmy Button and so many others died that the population was reduced from about 3000 to 2000 (according to estimates by the missionary Thomas Bridges). In 1881, the series uncontrolled epidemics began, lasted some twenty years and virtually exterminated the Yahgans as a viable population. An epidemic of measles followed, in 1925, and killed number of those who had managed to survive, including mestizos.

As of 1869 the Anglican missionaries applied a "double C strategy" (my term) - Civilize and Christianize. They did their utmost to convince the Yahgans, principally in the Ushuaia area, to abandon their way of living; moving constantly from one camp site to another, wearing scant clothing, living off nature, sharing anything available. The missionaries advocated: settling down in one place, in closed houses, cultivating gardens, tending sheep and cattle, if available, being responsible for self and family, not the community. They convinced many to don the second-hand clothing sent to the missionaries from London, Buenos Aires or Santiago, that unfortunately became disease carriers, to learn to eat vegetables (especially turnips), that is - become Civilized. Also they persuaded many to ignore their shamans, to forget the teachings of their elders, to give up their traditional ceremonies that is – adopt Christianity. "Civilization" made them more susceptible to the foreign diseases and "Christianity" demoralized many: the sacrifice of their entire tradition was too much to request and too abrupt. Previously the animals on which they had largely depended, seals and whales, had been largely depleted by the commercial fishing which began in the late eighteen century and continued into the twentieth (especially for seals). With the arrival of the Argentine navy and the government employees in 1884 prostitution was introduced and alcoholism became a mayor problem. Like the epidemics, the Yahgans (and Alakaluf) traditionally drank water so they had no "natural defense" against such beverages and were prone to become "drunk" more rapidly than the outsiders, with the result that violent quarrels among them were quit frequent and the men, who were more addicted to drinking excessively than the women, often abused their wives. The missionaries and the local Argentine government did their utmost to prohibit such drinking, but given the circumstances it became impossible to control.

The effects of the double colonization (religious and civil) virtually extinguished them as a people. By 1923 Gusinde calculated there were about seventy Yahgans including a few mestizos. But by 1933 there were only forty. This decline was partly due to the 1925 measles epidemic but also to the lack of fertility among the Yahgan women especially. Many of Yahgan men did not have wives. The surviving women had few children and some couples had none, even native women married to Argentines, Chileans or Europeans.[198]

The Yahgans had great difficulty adapting to the colonization that began in the 1870s. The colonizers, many from eastern Europe and some Chileans from Punta Arenas and later Argentines in Ushuaia, sought to exploit the seals, then gold, pastures for sheep and cattle, and lumber. Afterwards some industries, especially for marine products, were installed and finally tourism. The population of Ushuaia has grown from a few dozen Argentine men in 1884, the resident Yahgans, the missionaries and their families (a total of perhaps 200) to some 50,000 inhabitants in 2005. The population of 3,000 Yahgans, as estimated before the 1863 epidemic, has now declined to Cristina Calderon, who speaks the Yahgan language fluently, and whose both parents were Yahgan. She and quite a few Yahgan-mestizos live, in Villa Ukika, Puerto

23. My photograph of the late Ursula Calderón and her sister Cristina Calderón: Navarin Island, Chile, 1988.

Williams, Chile. The Chilean government has improved their living standard. The men work fishing or are employed in the local enterprises, as some of the women, while other women make the traditional baskets and miniature canoes to sell to tourists. Many cherish the memories that carry them back to lives full of emotions, many tragic but some happy and others inspiring. They and Cristina are working together with friends and colleagues in Chile and Argentina, to valorize and somehow vitalize their ancestral traditions.[199]

CHAPTER 6

BACK IN ENGLAND

The *Beagle* sailed through the recently surveyed Magdalena and Cockburn channels and entered the Pacific on June 10, 1834 and fifteen months later, on October 2, 1836 docked in Falmouth, near Plymouth. This part of the voyage is well known and easily accessible thanks to the many reprints of Darwin's *Voyage of the Beagle*, Richard Darwin Keynes's complete edition of his diary (1988), the very extensive Cambridge editions of his correspondence and the number of very readable recent books by British scholars noted above.

1. HOME AT LAST

Darwin: "On the 2nd of October we made the shores of England; and at Falmouth I left the *Beagle*, having lived on board the good little vessel nearly five years."[200] He headed home immediately.

Keynes explained:

> That same night, and a dreadfully stormy one it was, Charles took the mail coach home to Shrewsbury, where he arrived after two days on the road. After a joyful reunion with his father and sisters... [201]

And Janet Browne:

> He walked into The Mount [Shrewsbury], just before
> breakfast on Wednesday, 5 October, five years and three
> days after leaving home. "Why," said his father, "the shape
> of his head is quite altered."[202]

He visited his brother, Erasmus, in London, and then went to Cambridge to greet Professor Henslow, who had been such an essential friend and support during the long voyage. Back in London he met the great geologist, Charles Lyell. From then on, he contacted the variety of scientists involved with the specimens he had sent to Henslow, revised his diary for volume 3 as the *Narration...* later republished as *The Voyage of the Beagle* as mentioned above.[203]

He began writing a series of notebooks on geology at the end of June or in July 1837. Those labeled A and B were, as Browne pointed out, "his first halting works about evolution or transformism, as he tended to call it... [which] became the central, undisclosed hub of Darwin's life."[204] This is the beginning, or the continuation, of another "voyage" that culminated, twenty-two years later, with *On the Origin of Species...*

2. DARWIN'S FUEGIANS AND BEAGLE VOYAGE: 1871 AND 1876

In 1871 he recalled the Fuegians In *The Descent of Man...*

> They [the Fuegians-Yamanas] possessed hardly any arts,
> and like wild animals lived on what they could catch; they
> had no government, and were merciless to every one not
> of their own small tribe. He who has seen a savage in his
> native land will not feel much shame, if forced to acknowl-
> edge that the blood of some more humble creature flows
> in his veins.
> For my own part I would as soon be descended from that
> heroic little monkey who braved his dreaded enemy in
> order to save the life of his keeper or from that old
> baboon, who, descending from the mountains, carried

away in triumph his young comrade from a crowd of
astonished dogs-as from a savage who delights to torture
his enemies, offers up bloody sacrifices, practices infanti-
cide without remorse, treats his wives like slaves, knows
no decency, and is haunted by the grossest superstitions.
Man may be excused for feeling some pride at having
risen, though not through his own exertions, to the very
summit of the organic scale; and the fact of his having thus
risen, instead of having been aboriginally [sic] placed
there, may give him hope for a still higher destiny in the
distant future.[205]

This text reveals that Darwin's impressions of the Fuegians had
remained unchanged in 1871. His comparison of them with the heroic
little monkey and the courageous old baboon, should not surprise the
reader. He insisted on the biological and psychological continuity
among all species and particularly between humans and "lesser animals" such as monkeys and baboons. He also remained convinced that
humans had risen from merciless savagery, like that of the Fuegians, to
the "very summit of the organic scale."

But the above text also suggests that his attempt to apply the discoveries he made in *On the Origin of Species...* to *The Descent of Man...*
led to a contradiction, clearly implied in the last paragraph quoted
above. In this context a person's pride, however modest, logically cannot be derived from an event, or process, that was not, at least partially,
due to the person's "own exertions." We may congratulate each other for
having arrived at "the very summit of the organic scale" but we cannot
claim, according to Darwin, that it was through our "own exertions."

The Descent of Man... was yet another long "voyage." It has been
traced and extended by socio-biologists, mainly by E. O. Wilson, though
surely it has been interpreted and explained differently by other scholars.

In 1876 he wrote his last "homage" to the Beagle voyage, in his auto-
biographical notes (published in their original form thanks to Nora Barlow in 1958).

The voyage of the Beagle has been by far the most important event in my life and has determined my whole

career...I have always felt that I owe to the voyage the first real training or education of my mind...

Looking backwards I can now perceive how my love for science gradually preponderated over every other taste...the sense of sublimity, which the great deserts of Patagonia and the forest clad mountains of Tierra del Fuego excited in me, has left an indelible impression on my mind. The sight of a naked savage in his native land is an event which can never be forgotten.[206]

3. MY "HOMAGE" TO DARWIN

Darwin, seduced by the optimism of his social class, subscribed to the ideology or paradigm of cultural evolution which, combined with his too rapid and credulous impressions of the Fuegians (principally the Yahgan), gave him an erroneous and debasing image of them, despite his fondness for Jemmy Button and friendly relations with other Yaḥgans. Later, when confronted with opposition from most of the scientists of his time, he accepted the challenge of freedom and had the courage to carry out his prolonged research and publish his world-shaking theory on natural processes. This was indeed a noble and heroic venture.

4. FITZ-ROY'S CONTRIBUTIONS AND HIS "DESTINY"

He will certainly be long remembered for the care and consideration he took of the three Fuegians, York, Fuegia and Jemmy, and for having kept his promise to take them back to their homeland. After returning from his second Beagle voyage, he undertook the laborious task of compiling the first volume of the *Narrative of the Surveying voyages of H.M.S. Adventure and Beagle*, though it was partly written and signed by King. In 1839 Fitz-Roy completed his volume, the second, of the *Narrative...* and his *Sailing directions for South America*. He also checked the numerous coastal sheets, plans of harbors and views brought back from both voyages. These charts and his sailing directions were still in use in the 1970s. By then the Instituto Hidrográfico of the Chilean Navy began publishing a very extensive series of extremely detailed maps as well as sailing directions (*Derroteros*) that have finally outdated Fitz-Roy's. Darwin's granddaughter, Nora Barlow, was perhaps the first Darwin scholar who realized that Fitz-Roy had not received due recognition for his contributions.[207]

All of his adult life Fitz-Roy had been subject to periods of profound depression and in 1865 he committed suicide.[208]

Following his death, Darwin wrote in his memory:

> I never knew in my life so mixed a character. Always much to love & I once loved him sincerely, but so bad a temper & so given to take offence, that I gradually quite lost my love & wished only to keep out of contact with him. Twice he quarrelled bitterly with me, without any just provocation on my part. But certainly there was much noble & exalted in his character.[209]

5. AND THE *BEAGLE*

The "heroic little ship...the good little ship" was taken on an expedition to Australia the following year, under the command of Wickham. She then served as a coastguard and, from 1847 to 1870, as a "collier," transporting coal. Finally, as Keith Thomson discovered, at the age of fifty, she was ignominiously sold for scrap.[210]

NOTES

1. Gould. 1976.
2. It is perhaps time to mention the main sources I consulted for Darwin. In 1839 his text on the Beagle voyage appeared as volume 3 of the *Narration of the Surveying Voyages of H.M.S. Adventure and Beagle*. In 1845 he revised it and it was published as the *Journal of Researches into the Natural History*. This 1845 version has since been published in many editions with the title *The Voyage of the Beagle*. Sandra Herbert, an authority on Darwin's notebooks, stated (1974: 226): "It would be taking a misleadingly narrow view of what constitutes a scientific account to denigrate the Diary or the *Journal of Researches* on the grounds that they are popular works." Herbert's comment should suffice to justify treating *The Voyage of the Beagle* as well as his diary as authentic sources. I consulted the 1962 edition of the former. The complete text of Darwin's diary was published, in 1988, by Richard Darwin Keynes, Darwin's great grandson, therefore I use this edition instead of the 1933 edition by Norma Barlow, Darwin's diary granddaughter. The latter remains an important source because of her preface. Darwin also often mentioned Tierra del Fuego and the Fuegians in his correspondence published by Cambridge University Press, especially vol. I of 1985. I also consulted *On the Origin of Species...* (1859), *The Descent of Man...* (1871) and his autobiography, which he finished writing in 1876. Thanks to Nora Barlow, the latter in its original text was published in 1958. I also rely very much on the comments and analyses of Janet Browne: her two volume biography of Darwin, the first (1995) on his early life including the voyage, the second (2002) from then on to the very end of his life.

Desmond's and Moore's excellent biography of Darwin (1992) presents a somewhat different perspective than Browne's. The book by Alan Moorhead (1969) on the Beagle Voyage is well illustrated and original. Keynes, (1980 and 2003) mentioned above also offers fascinating accounts and analyses of Darwin's voyage. Herbert, who worked on Darwin's early notebooks (1974 and 1977), very recently (2005) published a long and detailed study of Darwin as a geologist. They all had access to documents which I was not able to consult. These are my main sources. I also use the works of many other scholars: biologists, anthropologists, historians of literature and science as well as the book by the explorer Eric Shipton (1979) because it is so clearly written. See the bibliography for the abbreviations I use in the notes that follow.

3. Browne 1995: 3-161; Desmond and Moore 1992: 5-97. The term Whig for a progressive political party may seem strange to non-British readers. According to *The Columbia Encyclopedia*: "It seems to have been a shorten form of *whiggamor* [cattle driver] and was used in the 17th century for Scottish dissenters."

4. Browne 1994; l995: 272; Keynes in CD Diary 1988: XX1-XX11.

5. CCD 1985 vol. 1: 142.

6. CD Autobio: 72; Browne 1995: 160. See Jonathan Miller's very easy reading and amusing introduction to Darwin, enhanced by the cartoons of Borin Van Loon (1982): p. 64 for the "nose scene".

7. Quoted from Clark (1984: 76) who did not name the son.

8. Also Clark 1984; 76; Browne 1995: 216-217; Degler (199l: 327) made this connection: "The growth of an animal rights movement has no obvious or direct connection with the revival of biology in the social sciences, but are not its intellectual springs to be found in the fateful continuity that Darwin discerned between animals and us?"

9. Browne 2002: 418-423, 486. Desmond and Moore observed (1992: 615): "Darwin was atypically British, an animal lover who loved his colleagues' autonomy more."

10. CD Beagle: 497-498.

11. CD Autobio.: 74; a letter to his sister Catherine CCD. vol. 1: 1985: 312-313; in his diary (1988: 45) though he did not mention the dispute with Fitz-Roy here it apparently took place on March 12, 1832 and again later. For Darwin on slavery see: Desmond and Moore 1992: 120-124; Browne 1995: 196-199; 2002: 214-216, 255-256.

12. Browne 1995: 246.

13. Desmond and Moore 1992: 231-232. Italics added.

14. I use the term Tierra del Fuego in its broadest connotation, to apply to all the islands south of the Magellan Strait to Cape Horn, though often it is only used for the Isla Grande. I also take the liberty of employing both generic names for the southern-most canoe people, Yamana as well as Yahgan. The most important general source for them is Gusinde 1986, in

Spanish, translated from the original in German of 1937. It was mostly but only partially translated, from German into English in 1961, therefore I have not used it. Wilbert (1977) translated most of the myths, also from the original German edition, into English. Thomas Bridges famous Yamana-English dictionary (1988) is an essential reference on innumerable subjects. His many articles in the Anglican mission magazine (published under three different titles from 1854 to the 1920s) can probably be found in the Library of Congress in Washington D.C. and the main British library in London. Easily available is his son's (Lucas Bridges 1987) fascinating biography of his family and himself with the Yahgans and Onas in Tierra del Fuego. Also available is McEwan *et al* (1997) that offers contributions from a variety of specialists on the glacial (pre-human) epoch, prehistory-archeology and essays on the native Fuegians known today. Cooper (1917) is essential. There are three important sources in French. A recent (1997) book presents articles on the French expedition to Cape Horn in 1882-83 and many of the photographs taken by two members of the expedition (in the bibliography, under the heading Cap Horn). Martial (1888) is the author of the first volume of this expedition and Hyades (1891), co-author with Deniker, of volume seven. Both are indispensable sources, as well as Hyades' other publications. In Spanish, Martinic B (2001) is very important. Two historical novels focus on Jemmy Button are very instructive: Subercaseaux (first edition 1950) and Canclini 1998. For the Alakaluf in English see Bird 1946 and Furlong 1917a, Emperaire 1955 and Laming 1954 in French and Wegmann's historical novel 1976 in Spanish. The main sources for the Selk'-nam are again Gusinde of 1982, translated into Spanish from the German original of 1931 (there is no English translation of this work) and Lucas Bridges 1987, mentioned above. John Cooper's article "The Ona," 1946 is very useful. My book in English, 1982, is out of print though available in some libraries. My other studies in English on the Selk'nam, were published in 1997, 2003a and b, On the Haush Indians there is far less because they were not always clearly distinguished from the their neighbors the Selk'nam, as in Gusinde 1982. For the Haush in English see also my article with Hester 1975, and Chapman 1982, chapter 2 and 2003b, chapter 8. There are a great many publications on archaeology of Tierra del Forego, both from Chile and Argentine. Several are cited in the text.

15.   Fuegia's mother was Yahgan though her father was Alakaluf. To make a long story short, Fitz-Roy took her as a prisoner with other members of her family or "tribe" and kept her as a hostage, in March 1830, (for the whaleboat the Alakaluf had stolen), when she was living in her father's territory near the island to be named Basket. She and the island were named Basket because Fitz-Roy's men, who were stranded on that island after their whaleboat was stolen, fashioned a craft with reeds, a

sort of basket, in which two of the men managed to return to the *Beagle*. Fitz-Roy reported that Fuegia's real name was Yokcushlu (or Yorkicushlu). However, I question the authenticity of this name simply because it looks like *york* plus *cushlu*, perhaps meaning the wife of York, that she was to become. York Minster was named after a cliff on Waterman Island, so-called by Captain James Cook during his second great voyage (in December 1774) because it reminded him of a large church or the cathedral (a minster) in his hometown of York. York Minster was Fitz-Roy's second hostage. He was captured, near that cliff, on Waterman Island, also in March 1830. One of his native names was El'leparu or Elleparu.

16. L. Bridges 1987: 30.

17. FR 1839: 12, 16.

18. CD Beagle 231.

19. *Ibid.*

20. See the anthropologist Alland 1985. Nevertheless, another anthropologist, Marvin Harris (1968:122) described Darwin as a racist mainly because of his attitude towards the Fuegians. But, the late Carl Sagan (1977: 6, 191-192), a highly esteemed authority on astronomy and space sciences, found "some justification" in the manner which Darwin derided the Fuegians. The anthropologist Boon (1983: 41) contested Sagan's "evolutions opinions". Richard Lee Marks 1991 whose "three men" in the title of his book are Fitz-Roy, Darwin and Jemmy Button, seemed to be carried away by his flair for writing. In any event, he made many absurd remarks about the Yahgans (on pp. 14-15, 31, 53, 73, 221-223, 225).

21. George W. Stocking Jr. an outstanding historian of anthropology, noted (1968: 113) that the concept of cultural evolution entered the academic domain thanks to three British anthropologists; John Lubbock, Darwin's good friend and neighbor, who began publishing in 1865, Edward Tylor and John McLennan who published a few years later. For influence of the cultural evolution concepts on Darwin see Herbert 1974: 225-229: Desmond and Moore 1992: 556: Bowler 1996: 181, and Browne 2002: 254-255.

22. Burrow 1968: 276. My source for the origins of our industrial-market society is Polanyi 1957. Henrika Kuklick (1991:116-117) should also be quoted here: "...evolutionist reasoning proved remarkably durable [in Victorian Britain] because it was incorporated in conventional wisdom. Survivals of unilinear, teleological developmental notions persist today in observations made everyday in ordinary situations...The folk anthropology of other parts of the industrialized West is much the same."

23. Browne 1995: 248-253. My comments on our industrial society are largely based on Polanyi 1957.

24. Gould 1977: 37-38; Browne 1995: 363.

25. In Gould's voluminous work, published shortly before he died, he dedicated almost fifty pages (2002: 952 to 999) to his approach to culture change.

26. CD Diary 1988: 3-7; Bowlby 1991: 124.

27. F-R 1839: 11,16; Desmond and Moore 1992: 111.

28. CD Diary 1988:133.

29. Diamond 1999: 246.

30. CD Beagle: 442; CCD 1991, vol. 7: 491, note 6.

31. FR 1839: 78; CD Beagle: p. XXIII; Browne 1995: 279; Desmond and Moore 1992: 130: Fitz-Roy (1839: 18-22) gave the names of many more.

32. CCD 1985 vol. 1: 472 in a letter to his sister Caroline; also Browne 1995: 312.

33. CCD 1985 vol. 1: 315 note 1, 393, 472, 549-551, 611-661; FR 1839: 19-21; Browne 1995; *passim*: see index; Desmond and Moore 1992 *passim*;; Moorehead 1985: 26; Thompson 1995: 92,156; Barlow 1933: XX1-XX111. See Keynes (1980 and 2003) for reproductions of Martens' unpublished drawings.

34. Herbert 1974: 225.

35. Browne 2002: 6,7,54.

36. Gould 1977: 141.

37. See Herbert's recent book *Charles Darwin, Geologist*, 2005 also Browne 1995: 186. Keynes (2003: 59) pointed out that Darwin inscribed in Lyell's volume one, "Given me by Capt. F.R. [signed] C. Darwin". Henslow sent him Lyell's second volume, which he received in Montevideo, in November 1832. Browne (1995: 338) explained how Darwin improved upon and supplemented Lyell's tenants. Also, according to Desmond and Moore (p.131) Lyell's second volume (*Elements of Geology*) was "curiously different from the first." Where as in the first he had dealt with gradual geological changes in the second he "asked whether animals and plants had been modified to match. Was there a natural mechanism for slowly transforming them to keep pace? No, was the [Lyell's] short answer." Darwin disagreed. His answer was long and was "yes."

38. For accounts of these trips and excursions see Browne 1995, Desmond and Moore 1992, Keynes 1980 and 2003 and Moorehead 1985.

39. Herbert 1974: 227.

40. CD Beagle: 207-208; not in CD Diary 1988. Twenty-one years later, in 1855, Captain W. Parker Snow (1857: vol. 2 37-38) found Jemmy in his home territory and hoped to take him to the Anglican mission station, recently established on the Falkland Islands. Snow, the first white man, to meet Jemmy, since Fitz-Roy and Darwin departed in 1834, showed Jemmy the above portrait and others drawn by Fitz-Roy. Snow commented: "The portraits of himself and the other Fuegians made him [Jemmy] laugh and look sad alternately, as the two characters he was represented in savage and civilized, came fore his eyes. Perhaps he was calling to mind his combed hair, washed face, and dandy dress, with the polished boots it is said he so much delighted in; perhaps he was asking himself which, after all, was the best, - the prim and starch, or the rough and shaggy? Which he thought he did not choose to say; but which I inferred he thought was gathered from his refusal to go anywhere [to the Falkland Islands] again with us [the British]." See also Mason 2001: 22-38, 51-54.

41. FR 1839: 119.

42. These days in Good Success Bay, 17-20 December 1832, are reported in CD Beagle: 204-211; CD Diary 1988; 121-128 and FR 1839:120-122. Apparently most of the "interaction" took place on 18 December.

43. Fitz-Roy wrote that five or six men greeted them while according to Darwin there were four.

44. Lucas Bridges (1987: 443) convincingly presented the basis for the hypothesis of the early arrival of the Haush from mainland Patagonia. Archaeologists working in the area do not necessarily accept this hypothesis, partly because the archaeological evidence of the Haush and the Selk'nam, comprised namely of instruments, traces of habitats and residues, are very similar, if not identical. Therefore it is very difficult, if not impossible, to distinguish one group from the other.

45. Browne (1995: 240-241) described the opera, by the German composer Weber, and added this significant comment: "Weber, not *Paradise Lost*, provided the analogy for the supernatural other-world of his Fuegian experience." Browne referred to Milton's *Paradise Lost*, because it was one of two books Darwin had brought along to read for pleasure. The other, by Alexander von Humboldt, was his favorite. This incident and the opera are also mentioned in Desmond and Moore 1992: 133.

46. The anthropologist, Michael Taussig (1997), in an original and inspired essay, cited this Darwinian scene, on the theme of the mimetic faculty, that he placed in a broad panorama which included Theodore Adorno, Antonio Artaud, George Bataille, Walter Benjamine, Emile Durkheim... to mention a few Taussig cited, in alphabetical order.

47. Even though the Haush language is not well documented, it is known to have been entirely different from the Yamana and Alakaluf languages. However, as these three groups shared certain customs, including repulsion of face hair, so the slightest gesture, body language, on the part of the old Haush man was certainly sufficient to convey the intended meaning to York and Jemmy.

48. In CD Beagle December 18 and 19 are not clearly distinguished. December 20 is mentioned, as above, in his diary 1988: 128.

49. CCD 1985 vol. 1: 306-307.

50. CCD 1985 vol. 1: 303.

51. CCD 1985, vol.1: 316.

52. CCD 1985 vol. 1: 397 (a letter to Charles Thomas Whitley).

53. CD Beagle: 501 See Street (1975: l0, 68) for his comments on the concepts of the "savage" in English fiction.

54. CD Descent: 1981 vol. 2: 404.

55. CD Autobio.126

56. It may be of interest to the reader to compare Darwin's comments about the Haush with Captain Cook's (in Beaglehole 1968: 44-45) of the thirty or forty Haush he encountered on January 16, 1769. Cook concluded his description, as Darwin might have: "In a Word they are perhaps as miserable a set of People as are this day upon Earth."

57. See Chapman 2003b Chapter 8 for an account of my hike through this area in 1970.

58. CD Beagle: 211.

59. CD Diary 1988: 127.

60. CD Diary 1988: 128.

61. FR 1839: 123-124; CD Beagle: 212 -217; CD Diary 1988: 128-130; Keynes 1980: 100-101: Keynes 2003: 125-126.

62. His diary reveals that while some of chapter ten describes impressions of the area visited or seen during that week, most were copied from his diary, or were impression of the experiences, in Yamana territory from January 19 to 28 (1833), when he, Fitz-Roy and others sailed and rowed through Beagle Channel and spent a week in Wulaia (Jemmy's territory), and February 6 when they returned to Wulaia. This chapter ten also includes notations made during the following year, February 26-27 (1834), when they went ashore on Wollaston Island, near Cape Horn (narrated below in chapter 4). He also noted here, in chapter ten, other information he obtained from Fitz-Roy and from William Low, a Scottish sealer, who spent many years in the area, whom he first met on Falkland Islands in March 1833.

63. Legoupil's expedition, in 1991, was the first mayor effort to survey the Cape Horn area. The results were published in 1995. The above date was given as 1410 BP (Before the Present, before 1991) that corresponds to approximately 580 A.D. with a margin of error of 60 years.

64. CD Beagle: 212-213; less details in CD Diary 1988: 222-224. See this entire quote from Stocking (1987: 106) and his analyses Darwin's concept of race and culture.

65. CD Beagle: 212.

66. Spegazzini 1882: 163.

67. CD Descent: vol. 1: 137.

68. Hyades (1891:345) wrote: "Fuegians" (the Yamana) carry fire everywhere they go and try not to let it extinguish "although they can ignite easily by sparks of iron pyrite, which are produced by the shock (impact) of one piece of mineral against another." Some other references are Cooper 1917: 191-192; Gusinde 1986 vol. 1: 377-379; Hyades 1891: 10; Martial 1888: 202: Webster 1970: 184.

69. According to *The Encyclopedia Britanica* (15th ed. 1983 vol. 8) pyrite contains 46.7 % iron and 53.33 % sulfur. The pyrite must be struck against a very hard metal (or stone containing one) in order that the tiny particles of pyrite (that result from this strike) liberate their sulfuric gas that thus produces "white heat" and a spark. *The Columbia Encyclopedia* (p. 975) stated that iron "is a prehistoric discovery [and] is chemically active and displaces the hydrogen in hydrochloric and sulphuric acids."

70. Gusinde 1982 vol.1: 188-89: 1986, vol. 1: 378.

71. L. Bridges 1987: 64.

72. CD Beagle: 212; CD Diary 1988: 130.

73. CD Beagle: 213.

74. For instance Fogg (1990; 28) noted "The fur rush in the Antarctic ended as suddenly as it had begun. By 1829, it was said, there was not a fur seal to be seen in the South Shetlands."

75. FR 1848:153; CD Beagle: 212.

76. Cooper (1917; 30) referred to the Chonos as; "The canoe-using Indians of the Chilean Channels who inhabited the area approximately from the Gulf of Peñas north to Guaitecas Islands. They were the northern neighbours of the Alakalufs."

77. CD Beagle: 214. Not mentioned in CD Diary 1988.

78. L. Bridges 1987: 81, note l.

79. FR 1839: 2, 462.

80. CD Beagle: 214-215.

81. CCD vol. 1: 304-. Desmond and Moore (1992: 569-570) contrast Darwin's attitude with Wallace's (who also "discovered" natural selection) who had said, while living with the native Dyaks in Borneo: "The more I see of uncivilized people, the better I think of human nature."

82. According to Romilly in CCD vol.1: 526 note l. italics in the original; also Browne 1999: 127, 352.

83. *On the Origin of Species...* 1995: 36.

84. CD Beagle: 208 215, 228: Fitz-Roy (1839: 183,189) clarified that Low's informant, the "native boy" a Chono from the region north of the Alakaluf territory, was known as Bob among the sealers, had never been south of Magellan Strait before he embarked with Captain Low. He told the same story as Jemmy Button, imitating "the piercing cries of the miserable victims whom he had seen sacrificed." Fitz-Roy added that Bob had recited his horrible story as a great secret and "seemed to be much ashamed of his countrymen, and said, he never would do so - he would rather eat his own hands. When asked why the dogs were not eaten, he said 'Dog catch iappo (otter)'. York told me that they [the Alakaluf] always eat enemies whom they killed in battle; and I have no doubt that he told me the truth." Fitz-Roy recalled that this accusation had been told to him by Jemmy and York on the *Beagle* and by "many different persons" as proof "that they eat human flesh...namely when excited by revenge or extremely pressed by hunger."

85. L. Bridges 1987: 33-36, 166-67. Most of the authorities on the Fuegians refuted Fitz-Roy's and Darwin's statements concerning cannibalism: Thomas Bridges in *Voice for South America*, vol. 13, 1866; also in *Buletino de la Sociedad de Geografia Argentina*, tomo 7, 1886.
Hyades 1891: 257-259; Gusinde 1986 vol. 1: 240-249; Lothrop 1928: 18; Cooper 1917: 194-195.

86. Engel in CD Beagle: 214, note 4.

87. L. Bridges 1987: 34.

88. CD Beagle: 216.

89. FR 1839: 179, 183.

90. Lumsden and Wilson 1983: 160, 163.

91. Hyades 1991: 374. Gusinde (1986 vol. 2:95- 959) also insisted on the Yamana's "sensibility" and their proclivity to become offended. He questioned the data of two murders a year.

92. Gusinde 1986 vol. 3: 1074-1111; Furlong 1909.

93. CD Beagle: 215 - 216. On the latter page he cited York again in an obscure story about his brother who killed a "wild man", and a storm raged as if to avenge the man's murder.

94. CD Descent: vol.1: 182,184 and vol. 2: 395.

95. See Wilbert 1977 for a translation and analyses of the Yamana myths published by Gusinde.
Gusinde 1986: vol. 3: 1065-69.

97. CD Beagle: 216; Gusinde 1986: vol. 1: 187-188; vol. 3: 1234-49; 1359-1412.

98. CD Descent vol. 1: 181.

99. CD Diary 1988: 141.

100. CD Diary 1988: 385; Gusinde 1986 vol. 2: 771-929 and Chapman 1997.

101. CD Beagle: 217; Hyades 1884: 558-559.

102. CD Beagle: 217.

103. Street 1975: 6. For their "non-perfectible canoe" see Chapman 2003c.

104. CD Beagle: 217.

105. CD Beagle: 217.

106. CD Descent: vol. 1: 34, 232.

107. Mayr 1995: p. IX.

108. FR 1839: 124.

109. CD Beagle: 218; CD Diary 1988: 133; CCD 1985 vol. 1: 303 a letter to his sister Caroline.

110. FR 1839: 125-126; CD Beagle: 218.

111. CD Diary 1988: 132; CD Beagle: 218.

112. CCD 1985 vol. 1: 316.

113. FR 1839: 126-127: FR in Keynes 1980: 163.

114. FR 1839: 127. According to Darwin (CD Diary: 133) they numbered twenty-eight. However, he didn't name the officers nor did he give the number of the crew while Fitz-Roy did.
115. FR 1839: 202-203.
116. CD Beagle: 218.
117. CD Beagle: 219
118. CD Diary 1988: 134; FR 1839: 203.
119. CD Beagle: 219 and CD Diary 1988:134.
120. FR 1839: 203: Sulivan (in *South American Missionary Magazine* 1881:131) quoted Thomas Bridges with the above translation though this expression, spelt in a variety of ways, is not in Bridges' dictionary (1987: 638-644).
121. CD Diary 1988: 134 and CD Beagle 220-221; FR 1839: 203-204.
122. CD Beagle: 221; CD Diary 1988; 135.
123. The reader of Darwin should be aware that he invariably called Murray Narrows "Ponsonby Sound" even though Fitz-Roy had already used the name Murray Narrows, as it appears on all the maps. Murray Narrows (eight miles long) flows into Ponsonby Sound at its southern extremity, in the vicinity of Button Island. It was named for Lord Ponsonby, the British Minster in Buenos Aires from 1826 to 1828, whom Fitz-Roy had probably met in Buenos Aires in 1828.
124. FR 1839: 204. Recall that neither Fitz-Roy nor Darwin used the terms Yahgan or Yamana and referred to them as Fuegians or Tekeenica.
125. FR 1839: 181, 204: CD Diary 1988: 137.
126. FR 1839: 205.
127. CD Beagle: 221.
128. FR 1839: 205-206, Gusinde (1986 vol. 2: 231-232 and note 315) thought that Jemmy's accounts were false, However, Cooper (1917: 196) asserted "that the Onas occasionally ventured and venture on the water is well enough attested." Jemmy's testimony is repeated so often in different contexts that it rings true.
129. FR 18839: 206-207; CD Beagle: 222.
130. CD Beagle: 222. Wulaia, Lewaia and Ushuaia are among the few localities whose original Yamana names have been respected. A favorite pastime of the explorers, the missionaries and later visitors was bestowing names on topographical features that caught their attention. The names were usually those of the members of an expeditions and friends, localities in their faraway homelands, or a faithful vessel such as that given to the great channel, in honor of the *Beagle*. The people who now live in Tierra del Fuego do not know most of the ancient Yahgan names. We are still far from documenting all those that have been published although a number of articles have appeared on the subject.
131. FR 1839: 208-209.
132. CD Beagle: 222-223; CD Diary 1988: 137.

133. Fitz- Roy (FR 1839: 209) placed the reunion of Jemmy with his family, the day of their arrival in Wulaia, January 23, while Darwin (CD Beagle: 223) stated that it occurred the following day which is more likely.
134. CD Diary 1988: 137.
135. FR 1839: 209; CD Beagle 223.
136. FR 1839: 210; CD Beagle: 223; CD Diary 1988: 137.
137. CD Beagle: 223. Not mentioned in his diary or by Fitz-Roy.
138. FR 1839: 210.
139. FR 1839: 211: L. Bridges 1987: 36.
140. CD Beagle 223 and CD Diary 138: F-R 1839: 213.
141. F-R 1839: 213.
142. CD Beagle: 223; CD Diary 138; FR 1839: 210-211.
143. F-R 1839: 212-213.
144. CD Diary 1988:138; also CD Beagle 224.
145. FR 1839: 212; CD Beagle: 224; CD Diary 138.
146. CD Beagle: 224.
147. CD Diary 1988: 138; FR 1839: 214.
148. CD Beagle: 224.
149. FR 1839: 214.
150. CD Beagle: 224.
151. FR 1839: 215.
152. CD Beagle: 224-225; CD Diary 1988: 139.
153. CD Beagle: 225.
154. FR 1839: 216.
155. FR 1839: 216; Derrotero (Sailing Directions) 1973: 144, 167: CD Beagle: 225.
156. FR 1839: 217; CD Beagle: 225-226.
157. FR 1839 217-219; CD Beagle: 226; CD Diary 1988: 140-141; Derrotero 1973: 394. To this day the Northwest Arm is preferred to the other arm, for its scenic beauty and because it is the most convenient route between Beagle Channel and the Strait of Magellan.
158. FR 1839: 219-220.
159. FR 1839: 138-139.
160. FR 1839: 220.
161. FR 1839: 220-221.
162. CD Beagle: 226-227; FR 1839: 221-222.
163. FR 1839: 222.
164. CD Diary 1988: 141,143. Italics added.
165. CD Beagle: 227.
166. FR 1839: 222; CD Beagle: 227.
167. FR 1839: 222-223.
168. FR 1839: 224-225; also Shipton 1973: 103. Not in Darwin because he had left Wulaia on February 6.
169. CD Diary 1988: 143-144.

170. CD Beagle chapters 3 to 9: CD Diary 1988: 144-217; Browne 1995: 254-268; Desmond and Moore 1992: 139-145; Moorehead 1988; chapters 6 to 8; Keynes 2003: chapters 10 to 14.

171. Jean-Paul Duviols ("The Patagonian 'Giants' "in McEwan *et al* 1997: 127-139) concluded his article with this phrase: "Thus by the end of the eighteenth century, this durable myth of [Patagonian] giants had finally been laid to rest."

172. FR 1839: 322.

173. CD Beagle 233: CD Diary 1988: 217-218.

174. CD Beagle 234. J.B. Hatcher, who published an excellent article on the Princeton University expedition to Patagonia in 1896-97, related the amazing impact the horse had made on the Tehuelches. "Not only was the advent of the horse the determining factor in supplanting the bow and arrow by the bola among these Indians, but the introduction of that useful animal produced other most decided changes in the life and habits of the Tehuelches."

175. CD Diary 1988: 218-220; FR 1839: 322; Moorehead 1987: 217.

176. CD Diary 1988: 221: Fitz-Roy (1839: 323) does not mention this incident.

177. CD Beagle: 233; CD Diary 1988: 221.

178. CD Diary 1988: 222.

179. CD Beagle: 213: CD Diary 1988: 222-224.

180. CD Beagle 227-228; CD Diary 1988: 224; FR 1839: 323.

181. CD Beagle: 228; CD Diary 1988: 226.

182. See my article on barter: Chapman 1980.

183. CD Beagle: 229; not in his diary.

184. CD Beagle: Ch. 10: 228-231, 233-234; CD Diary 1988: 2217-227: FR 1839: 322-332; Moorehead 1988: 217. For Mrs. Snow see Snow 1857 in the bibliography. A French woman, Rosa Freycinet, disguised herself as a man sailed around the world with her husband, Captain Louis de Freycinet. They came through or around Tierra del Fuego in 1820 but apparently neither she nor the crew went ashore.

185. FR 1839: 323.

186. CD Beagle: 229; CD Diary 1988: 226; Fitz-Roy 1839: 323-324.

187. CCD 1985: 380.

188. FR 1839: 325.

189. CD Beagle: 229-230; CD Diary 1988; 227; Fitz-Roy 1839: 325-326.

190. F-R 1839: 327.

191. CD Beagle: 230.

192. Eiseley 1961: 265.

193. CD Diary 1988: 240; CD Beagle 234-235.

194. CD Beagle 235.

195. CD Diary 1988: 241. These incidents are not mentioned in Fitz-Roy (1839: 358-359).

196. Personal communication from the linguist Oscar Aguilera (2001) who has been working among the Kaweskars for many years.

197. The anthropologist Marshall Sahlins (1972: 2-9) proposed that they had "original affluent society." Such analyses depend on how the negative and positive factors are weighed. The positive seemed dominant for Sahlins, who followed Gusinde, as it does for me. The point being made is that the Fuegians, as hunters/gatherers, were not poverty stricken "savages" on the outer edges of civilization. They had relatively well-balanced societies, from which a great deal can be learned today, for instance by comparing the Yahgan society to a general outline or model of our industrial society. Another anthropologist, Carleton Coon, stated (1971: 52): "One of the brightest men that our civilization has given birth to, Charles Darwin, considered the Yahgans to be the most brutish and debased people on the earth. As the examples of their technical skills cited [in Coon's book] show...that judgment was probably the most erroneous he ever made..."

198. Martinic 2001, especially pp. 21-27: Barclay 1926, 1987; Gusinde 1986 vol.1: 225, 327-350; Hyades 1886 and 1891.

199. See for example Stambuk 1986 (also translated into English); Alien 1995: Zárraga 2005: editor of stories told to her by Cristina and Ursula Calderon (bilingual: Spanish and English): Maurice von de Mire (in press).

200. CD Beagle 498.

201. Keynes 2003: 374.

202. Browne 1995: 340.

203. Browne 1995: 348: Herbert 1974: 245-258; 1977: 178; Desmond and Moore 1992: chapters 14 and 15.

204. Browne 1995: 363; Herbert 1974: 233-245: 1977: 184-185. For reproductions and analyses of his notebooks see Barrett *et al* 1987.

205. CD Descent: 1981 vol. 2: 404-405.

206. CD Autobio: 76-80.

207. Barlow 1933: p. XVI: Mellersh 1968 and Nichols 2003.

208. According to Desmond and Moore (1992: 104) Fitz-Roy had "feared his own hereditary disposition." In 1822 his uncle Viscount Castlereagh had slit his throat in a state of deep depression.

209. This passage is quoted in Desmond and Moore 1992: 530.

210. Thomson 1975 and 1998: 269.

BIBLIOGRAPHY

ABBREVIATIONS

CCD: Burkhardt, Frederick and Sydney Smith (eds.), *The Correspondence of Charles Darwin* (13 volumes from 1985 to 2002), Cambridge University Press, UK.

CD Autobio: Barlow, Autobiography of Charles Darwin, 1958.

CD Beagle: Darwin, Charles *The Voyage of the Beagle* (from the 1860 edition) L. Engle (ed. and introduction), 1962.

CD Descent: Darwin, Charles *The Decent of Man and Selection in Relation to Sex* (revised edition).

CD Diary 1933: Barlow, Nora (ed.) *Charles Darwin's Diary of the voyage of H.M.S., "Beagle"*. Cambridge University Press, 1933.

CD Diary 1988: Keynes, Richard Darwin (ed.) *Charles Darwin's Beagle Diary*. Cambridge University Press, 1988 (the complet edition).

FR 1839: Fitz-Roy, Robert (editor and author most of the text) *Narrative of the Surveying Voyages of his Majesty's ships "Adventure" and "Beagle". Vol. 11. Proceedings of the Second Expedition, 1831-1836, under the command of Captain Robert Fitz-Roy*, London, 1839.

Hyades 1891: actually Hyades and Deniker 1891, as cited below.

PK 1839: Parker King, (Robert Fitz-Roy was the editor of the volume and author of much of this text even though King appears as the author.) *Narrative of the Surveying Voyages of his Majesty's ships "Adventure" and "Beagle". Vol. I. Proceeding of the First Expedtion, 1826-1830, under the command of Captain P. Parker King*. London, 1839.

PUBLICATIONS CITED

Note that I translated all the above texts in Spanish and French to English unless otherwise indicated and that a year in brackets placed before the year of a later edition of a publication, indicate the year of its first publication.

Aguilera F., Oscar. 2001 *Gramática de la Lengua Kawésqar*, LOM Ediciones Ltda, Santiago, Chile.

Alland Jr., Alexander.1985 *Human Nature: Darwin's View*. Columbia University Press.

Aylwin Oyarzún, José.1995 *Comunidades Indígenas de los Canales Australes: Antecedentes Históricos y Situación Actual*. Arena Impresores, Santiago, Chile.

Barclay, William S.1926 *The Land of Magellan*. London.
1987 Preface IX-XX in Bridges, Thomas, 1987.

Barlow, Nora (ed. and author of Preface).1933 *Charles Darwin's Diary of the voyage of H.M.S. "Beagle."*Cambridge University Press, UK.
1958 *The Autobiography of Charles Darwin 1809-1882*. (With the original omission restored.) W. W. Norton Co. New York.

Barrett, Paul H., Peter J. Gautrey, Sandra Herbert, David Kohn & Sydney Smith. 1987 *Charles Darwin's Notebooks 1836-1844*. Ithaca, New York.

Beaglehole, John C. (ed. and author).1968 *The Journals of Captain James Cook on his Voyages of Discovery. The voyage of the Endeavour 1768-1771*. Cambridge University Press, UK

Billinghurst, Jean. 2000 *The Spirit of the whale. Legend, history, conservation*. Grantown on Spey, Scotland.

Bird, Junius. 1946 "The Alacaluf." *Handbook of South American Indians, Smithsonian Institution, Bureau of American Ethnology*, Bulletin 143,vol. I: 55-79.

Boon, James A. 1983 *Other tribes, other scribes. Symbolic anthropology in the comparative study of cultures, histoires, religions, and texts*. Cambridge University Press, Uc.

Borrero, Luis Alberto and Colin McEwan.1997 "The Peopling of Patagonia. The First Human Occupation." Chapter 2 in McEwan *et all* .

Bove, Giacomo.1883 *Expedición austral argentina. Informes preliminares presentados a S.S.E.E. los ministros del Interior y de Guerra y Marina de la República Argentina*. Published under the direction of the Instituto Geográfico Argentino, Buenos Aires.

Bowlby, John. 1991 *Charles* Darwin. A *new Life*, W.W. Norton & Co., New York.

Bowler, Peter J.1988 *The Non-Darwinian Revolution. Reinterpreting a historical Myth*. The Johns Hopkins University Press.
[1990]1996 *Charles Darwin. The man and his influence*, Cambridge University Press, UK.

Bridges, E. Lucas. [1948] 1987 *Uttermost Part of the Earth*, Century Hutchinson Ltd., London.

Bridges, Thomas. [1933] 1987 *Yamana-English: A Dictionary of the speech of Tierra del Fuego*. Dr. Ferdinand Hestermann and Dr. Martin Gusinde (eds.) includes a new preface by Natalie Goodall. Zagier y Urruty Publicaciones, Buenos Aires.

Browne, Janet.1994 "Missonaries and the human mind: Charles Darwin and Robert FitzRoy" in Macleod, and Rehbock (eds.): 263-279.

1995 *Charles Darwin Voyaging*. Random House, London.

2002 *Charles Darwin. The Power of Place*, Alfred A. Knopf, New York.

Burkhardt, Frederick and Sydney Smith (eds.).1985-2001 *The Correspndence of Charles Darwin*. 11 vols: 1985-2001 (consulted that cover the years 1821 to 1863). Cambridge University Press, UK. (More vols. have been published since 2001.)

Burrow, J.W. 1968 *Evolution and Society: a Study in Victorian social theory*. Cambridge University Press, UK.

Canclini, Arnoldo. 1998 *El fueguino. Jemmy Button y los suyos*. Editorial Sudamericana, Buenos Aires.

Cap Horn 1995 *Cap Horn. 1882-1883 Rencontre avec les Indiens Yahgan. Collection de la Photothèque du Musée de l'Homme*, Editions de la Martinière, Muséum National d'Histoire Naturelle, Photothèque du Musée de l'Homme, Paris.

Chapman, Anne. 1964-1988 *Diary of field work among the Selk'nam and Yamana* (Typescript).

1980 "Barter as a Universal Mode of Exchange." *L' Homme*, vol. XXI: 33-83.

1982 *Drama and Power in a Hunting Society. The Selk'nam of Tierra del Fuego*. Cambridge University Press, UK.

1987 *Isla de los Estados en la Prehistoria. Primeros datos arqueológicos*. EUDEBA, Buenos Aires.

1997 "The Great Ceremonies of the Selk'nam and the Yamana. A Comparative Analysis." Chapter 5 in McEwan *et al.*

2003a *Hain. Initiation Ceremony of the Selk'nam*. Taller Experimental Cuerpos Pintados, Santiago, Chile.

2003b *End of a World: the Selk'nam of Tierra del Fuego*. Taller Experimental Cuerpos Pintados, Santiago, Chile (second edition).

2003c *El Fenómeno de la Canoa Yagán*, Viña del Mar, Chile.

Chapman, Anne and Thomas R. Hester. 1975 "New Data on the Archaeology of the Haush: Tierra del Fuego," *Journal de la Société des Américanistes*, tome 62: 185-208.

Clark, Ronald W. 1984 *The Survival of Charles Darwin. A biography of a man and an idea*. Random House, New York.

Coon, Carleton S. 1971 *The Hunting Peoples*. Little, Brown & Co., Boston.

Cooper, John M.1917 "Analytical and critical bibliography of the tribes of Tierra del Fuego and adjacent Territory," *Smithsonian Institution, Bureau of American Ethnology*, Bulletin 63 Washington D.C.

1946 "The Yahgan" *Handbook of South American Indians, Smithsonian Institution, Bureau of American Ethnology*, Bulletin 143, Washington vol. I: 81-106.

Darwin, Charles (see Burkhardt and Smith for his correspondence; Barlow and Keynes for his diary; Barlow for his autobiograpy)

[1845] 1962 *The Voyage of the Beagle.* edited and Introduction by Leonard Engel, A Doubleday Anchor Book, The American Museum of Natural History.

[1871] 1981*The Decent of Man and Selection in Relation to Sex.* Introduction by John Tyler Bonner and Robert M.May, Princeton University Press.

[1859] 1995 *On the Origin of Species by Means of Natural Selection.* Introduction by Ernest Mayr, Harvard University Press.

Degler, Carl N.1991 *In Search of Human Nature*, Oxford University Press.

*Derrotero de la Costa de Chil*e [Sailing Directions] vol. V "Tierra del Fuego y Canales e Islas Adyacentes," 1973 (6th ed.) Instituto Hidrográfico de la Armada, Valparaíso, Chile.

Desmond, Adrian and James Moore. 1992 *Darwin.The Life of a Tormented Evolutionist.* W. W. Norton & Co. New York.

Diamond, Jared.1999 *Guns, Germs, and Steel. The Fates of Human Societies.* W.W.Norton & Co., New York.

Duviols, Jean-Paul.1997 "The Patagonian 'Giants' ." Chapter 7 in McEwan *et al.*

Eiseley, Loren. 1961 *Darwin's Century: Evolution and the man who discovered it.* Doubleday & Co., Garden City, New York.

Emperaire, José. 1955 *Les Nomades de la Mer.* Gallimard, Paris.

Encylopedia, Columbia University Press, 1950 (2nd edition).

Encylopedia Britanica, 1992 (15th edition).

Engel, Leonard. 1962 "Introduction" in Darwin *The Voyage of the Beagle* pp. IX-XXII.

Fanning, Edmund.1833 *Voyages round the world with selected sketches of voyages to the south seas, northern south Pacific oceans, China, etc.* Collins & Hannay, New York.

Fitz-Roy, Robert (editor of the 3 volumes of the *Narrative...* and author of vol. 2 below : see King, P. Parker 1839 for vol. 1 and Darwin, Charles 1962 a reprint of the second edition (1845) of vol. 3.

1839 "Narrative of the Surveying Voyages of his Majesty's ships 'Adventure' and 'Beagle', between the years 1826 and 1836, describing their examination of the southern shores of South America and the 'Beagle' circumnavigation of the globe." Vol. 2. *Proceedings of the Second Expedition, 1831-1836, under the command of Captain Robert Fitz-Roy,* London.

1848 *Sailing Directions for South America. Part II. La Plata, Patagonia, Falkland and Staten Islands, Chile, Bolivia and Peru.* London, printed by the Hydrographic Office, Admiralty, London.

Fogg, G.E. 1990 *The Explorations of Antarctica. The Last Unspoilt Continent.* Cassell, London.

Furlong, Colonel Charles Wellington. 1909 "The Southermost People of the World" *Harpers Monthly Magazine,* June: 120-134.

1917a "The Alaculoofs and Yahgans, the world's southernmost inhabitants" *Proceedins of the Nineteenth Interntional Congress of Americanists,* Washington D.C. : 320-431.

1917b "The Haush and Ona, primitive tribes of Tierra del Fuego" *ibid.:* 432-444.

Goodall, Rae Natalie Prosser. 1975 *Tierra del Fuego. Argentina,* Editiones Shanamiim, Buenos Aires.

1987 "Preface" in Thomas Bridges *Yamana-English. A Dictionary of the speech of Tierra del Fuego.*

Gould, Stephen Jay.1976 "Darwin and the Captain" *Natural History,* vol. 85, no. 1: 32-34.

1977 *Ever Since Darwin, Reflections in Natural History.* W.W. Norton, New York.

2002 *The Structure of Evolutionary Theory.* Harvard University Press.

Gusinde, Martin.1961 *The Yamana.* University of Michigan: in five Parts: a partial translation of *Die Feuerland- Indianer: Die Yamana.* Mödling, Viena 1937: also published by the Human Area Relations Files, Yale University Press.

1982 *Los Indios de Tierra del Fuego: vol. I, los Selk'nam.* 2 tomos. Centro Argentino de Etnología Americana, Buenos Aires. Originally published in one vol. as *Die Feuerland- Indianer: Die Selk'nam .* Mödling, Viena, 1931.

1986 *Los Indios de Tierra del Fuego. vol. II Los Yámana.* 3 tomos. *Ibid* (originally published in German, in 1937 as noted above).

Harris, Marvin. 1968 *The Rise of Anthropological Theory, a History of Theories of Culture.* New York.

Hatcher, J.B.1901 "The Indian Tribes of Southern Patagonia, Tierra del Fuego, and the Adjoining Islands" *The National Geographic Magazine,* vol. 12, no. 1: 12-22.

Herbert, Sandra. 1974 "The Place of Man in the Development of Darwin's Theory of Transmutation. Part I" *Journal of the History of Biology,* vol. 7, no. 2: 217-258.

1977. "The Place of Man in the Development of Darwin's Theory of Transmutation. Part II" *ibid.* vol. 10, no.2: 155-227.

2005 *Charles Darwin, Geologist.* Cornell University Press.

Hyades, Paul Daniel Jules. 1884 "Notes hygiéniques et médicales sur les Fuégiens de l'archipel du Cap Horn" *Revue d'Hygiène et de Police Sanitaire*, vol. VI: 550-59.

1886 "Les Epidémies chez les Fuégiens" *Bulletin de la Société d'Anthropologie. de Paris*, tome IX: 202-205 (includes letter from Thomas Bridges).

Hyades, P. D. J. and J. Deniker. 1891 "Anthropologie, Ethnographie" tome VII of the eight tomes or volumes of the *Mission Scientifique du Cap Horn 1882-1883*, Minsteres de la Marine et de l'Instructions Publique, Gauthier-Villars et Fils, Paris.

Keynes, Richard Darwin (author & ed.). 1980 *The 'Beagle' Record. Selections from the original pictorial records and written accounts of the voyage of H.M.S. Beagle.* Cambridge University Press, UK.

1988 *Charles Darwin's Beagle Diary.* Cambridge University Press, UK.

2003 *Fosils, finches and Fuegians. Charles Darwin's Adventures and Discoveries on the Beagle, 1832-1836*, Harper-Collins, London.

Kuklick, Henrika. 1991 *The savage within. The social history of British anthropology, 1885-1945.* Cambridge University Press, UK.

Kuhn, Thomas S. [1962] 1970 *The Structure of Scientific Revolutions.* Second edition, enlarged, The University of Chicago Press.

Laming, Annette. 1954 *Tout au Bout du Monde, avec les hommes et les betes en Patagonie.* Amiot-Dumont, Paris.

Legoupil, Dominique. 1995 "Les Indigènes au Cap Horn: Conquète d'un Territoire et Modèle de Peuplement aux Confins du Continent Sud-Américain," *Journal de la Société des Américanistes* tome 81: 9-45.

Lothrop, Samuel K. 1928 *The Indians of Terra del Fuego.* Museum of the American Indian, Heye Foundation, New York.

Lumsden, Charles J. and Edward O. Wilson 1983 *Promethen Fire, Reflections on the Origin of Mind.* Harvard University Press.

MacLeod, Roy and Philip E. Rehbock (eds.). 1994 *Evolutionary Theory and Natural History in the Pacific Darwin's Laboratory.* University of Hawa'i Press, Honolulu.

Marks, Richard Lee. 1991 *Three Men of the Beagle.* Alfred A. Knopf, New York.

Martial, Louis Ferdinand. 1888 "Histoire du Voyage" tome 1 of the eight tomes or volumes of the *Mission Scientifique du Cap Horn 1882-1883*, Minsteres de la Marine et de l'instructions Publique, Gauthier-Villars et Fils, Paris.

Martinic B., Mateo. 1982 *La Tierra de los Fuegos: Historia Geografía Sociedad Economia*, Municipalidad de Porvenir, Tierra del Fuego, Chile.

2001 "El Postrer Esfuerzo Misional entre los Yamana (1888-1917). Significación en la Decadencia Etnica, Estado de la Comunidad final (1918-2000)." *Anales del Instituto Patagonia*, Chile, vol. 29: 5-27.

Mason, Peter. 2001 *The Lives of Images.* Reaktion Books, London.

Mayr, Ernst.1988 *Toward a New Philosophy of Biology. Observations of an Evolutionist.* Harvard University Press.

1995 "Introduction" of *On the Origin of Species*, by Charles Darwin, pp. VII-XXVII. A facsimile of the first edition (1859), Harvard University Press.

McEwan, Colin, Luis A. Borrero and Alfredo Prieto (eds.). 1997 *Patagonia. Natural History, Prehistory and Ethnography at the Uttermost end of the Earth*, British Museum Press, London.

Mellersh, H.E.L. 1968 *Fitz-Roy and the Beagle*, Rubery Hart Davis Publishers.

Mena, Francisco. 1997 "Middle to Late Holocene Adaptations in Patagonia." Chapter 3 in McEwan *et all.*

Miller, Jonathan and Borin Van Loon. 1982 *Darwin for Beginners.* Pantheon Books, New York.

Moorehead, Alan. {1969} 1985 *Darwin and the Beagle* Harper & Row publisher, New York.

[1966] 1987 *The Fatal Impact. The Invasion of the South Pacific 1797-1840.* Mead & Beckett Publishing, Sydney, Australia.

Nichols, Peter. 2003 *Evolution's Captain. The tragic fate of Robert FitzRoy, the man who sailed Charles Darwin around the world.* Harper Colins Publishers Inc, New York.

Polanyi, Karl. [1944] 1957 *The Great Transformation*, Beacon Press, Boston.

Sagan, Carl . 1977 *The Dragons of Eden. Speculations on the Evolution of Human Intelligence.* Random House, New York.

Sahlins, Marshall.1972 *Stone Age Economies.* Aldine, Chicago.

Shipton, Eric. 1973 *Tierra del Fuego: the Fatal Lodestone.* London.

Slocum, Jochua. [1900] 1956 *Sailing Alone Around the World.* Cover Publications, Inc., New York.

Snow, W. Parker. 1857 *A Two Years Cruise off Tierra del Fuego, the Falkland islands, Patagonia and in the River Plate: a narrative of life in the southern seas.* 2 vols. London.

Spegazzini, Carlos. 1882 "Costumbres de los Habitantes de la Tierra del Fuego" *Anales de la Scoiedad Cientifica Argentina*, Tomo 14: 159-181.

Stambuk M., Patricia. 1976 *Rosa Yagán. El Ultimo Eslabón.* Editorial Andrés Bello, Santiago, Chile (published later in English).

Stocking Jr. George W.1968 *Race, Culture, and Evolution. Essays in the History of Anthropology.* The Free Press, New York.

1987 *Victorian Anthropology. Ibid.*

Street, Brian V. 1975 *The savage in literature. Representations of 'primitive' society in English fiction 1858-1920.* Routledge and Kegan Paul, London.

Subercaseaux, Benjamin. 1950 *Jemmy Button*, editions Ercilla, Chile.

Taussig, Michael.1997 "Tierra del Fuego – Land of Fire, Land of Mimicry. " Chapter 9 In McEwan *et al* .

Thomson, Keith Stewart. 1975 "H.M.S. Beagle 1820-1870" *American Scientist* vol. 63: 664-672.

1998 *H M S Beagle. The Story of Darwin's Ship*, W.W. Norton & Co., New York.

Webster, Dr W.H.B. [1834] 1970 *Narrative of a voyage to the Southern Atlantic Ocean, in the years 1828,29,30, performed in H.M.S. Sloop Chanticleer, under the command of the late Captain Henry Foster.* 2 vols. London.

Weddell, James. [1825] 1970 *A Voyage toward the South Pole, performed in the years 1822-24.* second edition with a new introduction by Sir Vivian Fuchs. London.

Wegmann, H., Osvaldo. 1976 *La Ultima Canoa.* 2 vols. Hersprint, Punta Arenas, Chile.

Wilbert, Johannes. 1977 *Folk Literature of the Yamana Indians. Martin Gusinde's Collection of Yamana Narratives.* University of California at Los Angeles Press.

Wilson, Edward O. (see above Lumsden and Wilson)

Zárraga, Cristina (ed.) 2005 *Hai kur mamashu shis (Quiere contarte un cuento)* (stories told to the editor by her grandmother Cristina Calderón and grandaunt Ursula Calderón, Spanish and English, Imprenta America, Valdivia, Chile.

LIST OF ILLUSTRATIONS

1.	Charles Darwin in 1840.	2
2.	Robert Fitz-Roy in 1858.	3
3.	York Minster in England.	19
4.	Fuegia Basket in England.	20
5.	Jemmy Button in England.	21
6.	Halimink in 1923.	23
7.	Good Success Bay in 1769.	26
8.	Guanacos, then and now.	34
9.	Wollaston islanders in 1834.	38
10.	A Yahgan man, rather recently.	41
11.	Scene of a beached whale in 1883.	45
12.	Yamanas painted for mourning, about 1922.	53
13.	A Yahgan family in their canoe probably about 1900.	59
14,	A Yahgan woman, rather recently.	61
15.	Wulaia in 1833.	79
16.	Wulaia off the shore in 1987.	81
17.	A. Chapman seated on whale bones, 1972.	107
18.	A. Chapman in Thetis Bay, 1969.	109
19.	The *Bealge* in Murray Narrows, 1834.	111
20.	A Yahgan man who looks like Jemmy Button, 1834.	114
21.	Jemmy and his family biding farewell to the *Beagle*, 1834.	119
22.	Joshua Slocum shooting towards the Alakaluf, 1896.	122
23.	Cristina Calderón and her late sister Ursula Calderón, 1987.	125

IMAGO MUNDI

Este libro se terminó de imprimir en EIM impresos,
Av. Independencia 3018 - Tel. (011) 4932-3890 - C1225AAZ
Ciudad Autónoma de Buenos Aires, e-mail: odilonlibros@fibertel.com.ar,
en el mes de abril de 2006.